A Journey
with
Two Maps

Eavan Boland

A Journey
with
Two Maps

Becoming a Woman Poet

W. W. NORTON & COMPANY

NEW YORK • LONDON

"Frühling 1946" © 1959 Elisabeth Langgässer, Claassen Verlag in der Ullstein Buchverlage GmbH, Berlin, reprinted courtesy of Ullstein Buchverlage GmbH. Excerpts from "The Pattern" and "The Statue of the Virgin at Granard Speaks" © Paula Meehan, reprinted by permission of Wake Forest University Press. Excerpts from "Another September" © Thomas Kinsella, Wake Forest University Press. Excerpts from "Candelight," "Nick and the Candlestick," and "Night Dancers" © 1960, 1965, 1981 by the Estate of Sylvia Plath. Editorial material © Ted Hughes, Reprinted by permission of HarperCollins Publishers. Excerpts from "Renascence," "Sonnet XLIII," "First Fig," "A Portrait by a Neighbor," "Daphne," and "Recuerdo" © 1917, 1922, 1923, 1945, 1950, 1951 by Edna St. Vincent Millay and Norma Millay Ellis, Reprinted with permission of Elizabeth Barnett, the Millay Society.

For information about permission to reproduce selections from this book, write to Permissions, W. W. Norton & Company, Inc., 500 Fifth Avenue, New York, NY 10110

For information about special discounts for bulk purchases, please contact W. W. Norton Special Sales at specialsales@wwnorton.com or 800-233-4830

Manufacturing by RR Donnelley, Harrisonburg

Book design by Brooke Koven

Production manager: Julia Druskin

Library of Congress Cataloging-in-Publication Data

Boland, Eavan.

A journey with two maps : becoming a woman poet / Eavan Boland. — 1st ed.

p. cm.

Includes index.

ISBN 978-0-393-05214-5

1. Boland, Eavan—Authorship. 2. Poetry—Authorship. I. Title.

PR6052.O35J68 2011

824'.914—dc22

2010054023

W. W. Norton & Company, Inc.

500 Fifth Avenue, New York, N.Y. 10110

www.wwnorton.com

W. W. Norton & Company Ltd.

Castle House, 75/76 Wells Street, London W1T 3QT

1 2 3 4 5 6 7 8 9 0

For Jody Allen-Randolph

CONTENTS

Destinations

ACKNOWLEDGMENTS

"Being an Irish Poet: The Communal Art of Paula Mee-
han" appeared in *An Sionnach: A Special Issue on Paula
Meehan*, edited by Jody Allen Randolph.
"The Case of Edna St. Vincent Millay" appeared in
Water~Stone Review.
"Charlotte Mew: An Introduction" appeared as the
introduction to *The Selected Poems of Charlotte Mew*,
edited by Eavan Boland (Carcanet Press, Manchester,
England).
"Domestic Violence" appeared in the *American Poetry
Review* and *PN Review.*
"Domestic Violence" and "Translating the Underworld"
were published, respectively, under the titles "My
Blue Piano" and "Frühling 1946" in *After Every War:
Twentieth-Century Women Poets*, edited by Eavan
Boland (Princeton University Press).
"Elizabeth Bishop: An Unromantic American" first
appeared in *Parnassus: Poetry in Review.*
"A Latin Poet: A Lost Encounter" appeared in a slightly
different form in *PN Review.*

"A Latin Poet: A Lost Encounter" was published under the title "Foebus Abierat" in *Poetry* magazine.

"Letter to a Young Woman Poet" appeared in *The American Poetry Review* and in *Feminist Literary Theory and Criticism: A Norton Reader,* edited by Sandra Gilbert and Susan Gubar (W. W. Norton & Company).

"Looking Back and Finding Anne Bradstreet" appeared in *Green Thoughts, Green Shades: Essays by Contemporary Poets on the Early Modern Lyric,* edited by Jonathan Post (University of California Press), and in *Seventeenth-Century British Poetry, 1603–1660* (Norton Critical Edition), edited by John P. Rumrich and Gregory Chaplin (W. W. Norton & Company).

"The Other Sylvia Plath" appeared in *The Grand Permission: New Writings on Poetics and Motherhood,* edited by Brenda Hillman and Patricia Dienstfrey (Wesleyan University Press).

"Translating the Underworld" appeared in *Northwest Review.*

THANKS TO THE editors of the journals and anthologies in which these essays appeared. Thanks to Kevin Casey, Jill Bialosky and Michael Schmidt.

Special thanks to my friends and colleagues at Stanford University.

PREFACE

THIS IS A BOOK OF being and becoming. It is about being a
poet. It is also about the long process of becoming one. If
these seem in the wrong order there is a reason: the disor-
der is part of my subject. There is nothing settled about a
poet's identity. The becoming doesn't stop because the being
has been achieved. They proceed together, attached in ways
that are hard to be exact about. For that reason, this is not a
scholarly book. I did not approach my subject by finding facts.
I approached it by finding myself.

"Ask yourself in the most silent hour of your night: must I
write?" said Rilke. Such clarity is hard to come by when you're
young. Poetry seemed a magisterial entity back then—not by
any means open to a question asked in the silent dark. To
start a poem on an ordinary Dublin afternoon was anything
but simple. I didn't know how to weigh ideas about poetry.
Nothing in the life I lived as a student—and later as wife and
mother at the suburban edge of Dublin—suggested I had the
wherewithal to do so.

But I did have a unit of measurement. It was the measure of my own life. It was there in the awkward and fanciful
assembly of myself as a woman poet in the powerful, resis-

tant literary culture I inherited. Looking back, it seems even now an impossible enterprise: like an early aviator in a remote place, hiding the bulky wings and small wheels in a garage or back garden to protect the odd, presumptuous dream of flight. I was the aviator. I assembled the dream slowly, over years. It was this which gave me some way of understanding my subject; and made this book.

Poetry begins where language starts: in the shadows and accidents of one person's life. And yet many traditional accounts of the making of a poet are over and done with before the reader gets there. Even though I admired those texts when I was young, I regretted they didn't wait for me. The growth of a poet's mind was written about—often with extraordinary power—at its finishing point rather than its source.

I locate those beginnings at an earlier stage here. I push the process back to an origin some may think too personal. But I wanted to write that record, for the very reason that it has often been unwritten. To do that I knew I needed an alternative critique, one that blended autobiography and analysis. Both seemed necessary. It seemed right that the intimacy and dailyness of experience not be separated from the rigors of criticism, if only because they co-exist in the life of a working poet. They certainly co-existed in mine.

"How shall we tell each other of the poet?" wrote Muriel Rukeyser. In the spirit of that question, the second part of this book is about women poets I've admired and learned from. When I was young some of them were unknown to me, even by name: nothing in my education had pointed me towards them. Because of that, a part of my formation happened without the light and example of some of these poems. And so it may be that the real editors of this book are passion and regret.

Once I began to read them, of course, these poets became a perspective on everything else. Long before I came to divide my time between California and Dublin I located myself on common ground: in American poetry as well as Irish, and British as well as American. The first women poets I found were from other countries. Their work filled up the silences that troubled me at home. In the sense that my life as a poet has been marked by boundaries, this book allows me to unwrite them—moving more freely between countries and poems and histories.

To mark my early discoveries, most of the poems here are not Irish. But I never forgot in reading them—not for one moment—that I was. I make it plain that I understood these texts again and again through my Irishness. They were most often observed through the lens of my life as a woman and poet in a small country most of their authors had never seen; and yet they helped me live it.

Both these parts of the book are held together by a single thread: I have come to believe the journey towards being and becoming a poet cannot happen with one set of directions only. Or, to use the figure I choose here, one map. It seems obvious that ideas of composition or canonicity should never be privileged over even one poem whose voice or style is a challenge. The poem takes precedence. And yet that very precedence can prove disruptive to previous understandings of poetry.

Therefore this book unfolds the idea of those two maps. I still believe many poets begin in fear and hope: fear that the poetic past will turn out to be a monologue rather than a conversation. And hope that their voice can be heard as that past turns into a future. The first map I followed included a detailed description of the past. The second one provided directions for the future of that voice, and for a new relation with that past.

In these essays, I try to explain exactly what these so-called maps meant to me personally: how at various times I looked at conflicting ideas of a poetic self and an inherited craft and was bewildered at how to balance my obligations to a poetic past with my need to write in the present tense, and out of my own life. And how in the end, for all the inherent contradictions I found, I determined to keep both maps; and to learn from both.

Finally, this book is a tribute to the richness and variety of women's poetry over the last century. I write this knowing the statement itself has built-in tensions. The very category of women poets can and does cause a frank unease. Some people propose it as inevitably reductive: an actual limitation in the way of seeing poetry. I have never shared this view. For me it overlooks something commonsensical. New voices in an old art—and women poets have been that for much more than a century—do not diminish the art through the category. They enrich it. They renew it with common quandaries of craft and innovation. The category simply allows the quandaries to be seen more clearly.

Far from expressing unease, these essays record my excitement at how Sylvia Plath re-stated the nature poem and Gwendolyn Brooks the urban lyric. At the way Elizabeth Bishop re-made the Romantic self and Adrienne Rich re-formed a civic art. Because of them, and others here, something happened for me that I am sure has happened for many readers: an apparently monolithic poetic past was transformed into a conversation I could join and change.

Eavan Boland
Stanford and Dublin, 2010

Journeys

A Journey with Two Maps

I

It might seem odd, even wrongheaded, to begin a book of criticism with a personal narrative. But I have a reason. A story makes a straight path through confusion. It clears the way. And the way needs to be cleared. It would be simpler for every poet if the ethics and aesthetics surrounding them were fixed and signposted. But they're not. Sometimes whatever clarity there is emerges only gradually out of human impulses, human flaws. This piece, very deliberately, is about such flaws; in this case my own. I found them out through a chance encounter; painful, telling and corrective. And since this book is about all the ways poets defy expectations, it seems right to begin with a story about the upending of my own.

My mother was my hero. Without that flat statement, this piece will have no meaning. As an awkward and displaced teenager I looked up to her. So much so that I made a skewed calendar in my mind: I measured history by her life. 1909, for instance—not the year of the Land Purchase Act but the time her mother died in a fever ward in Dublin. 1915. The year after the Great War started, yes. But more importantly, the year she was called out of class in the Dominican Convent in Dublin to be told her father had drowned in the Bay of Biscay. 1916. The year of the Irish Rising. But also the year she was made a ward of court.

And so it went on. 1928. Not the year of the first Censorship of Publications Act in Ireland. But the time she went to Paris to study art, sitting in the freezing air on the deck of a ferry to Le Havre. Year after year, I counted dates and shifted seasons. And in doing so I allowed the entirely personal to warp the truly eventful.

It wasn't logical. That much I knew. But I was a teenager newly returned to Ireland. The dates and events of its history had little hold on me. My mother's life did. It was her past, to use Elizabeth Bishop's eloquent description of travel, that seemed to me "serious, engraveable." Not the Irish one. And so, without knowing it, I stumbled on one of the essential timekeepers: A magic permission to make time a fiction and the imagined life a fact. A way, in other words, of making a visible history answer to a hidden life.

Two things shaped my relationship with my mother. First the wrenching facts of her life. Born of a mother who died at thirty-one in a fever ward. Of a father who drowned in the Bay of Biscay. Before she left her childhood she had lost most of what determines it for other people. She became a ward of court as a child. She appeared homeless to me; somehow unclaimed. Like Lorna Goodison's grandmother in her poem "Guinea Woman," her future was determined by losses: *It seems her fate was anchored / in the unfathomable sea.*

Second, and just as important, she was an artist. She began drawing and painting early. She left boarding school young. Eventually she went to the College of Art in the center of Dublin. There she won a scholarship, adjudicated by Yeats's friend A. E. Russell. It was called the Henry Higgins Scholarship. It took her to Paris for three years of instruction in the mid-1930s.

Paris was then a city full of studios and teachers. Most Irish art students ended up in the ateliers of teacher-artists like Henri Lhote. My mother did something different. She heard from a friend that a painter had a vacancy for a private student because his American pupil had gone back unexpectedly to the States. She asked him to take her as a replacement. He agreed.

I have some early press cuttings. They detail my mother's first exhibition in Dublin in 1936. By then she was a married woman. They are yellowish and crisp now. And so I have to imagine them in their original context: small, exciting notes in the folded evening newspaper of a provincial city. I have to imagine the convivial gallery party. Feathered hats and macabre furs. The half-column in the *Evening Herald* states below her photograph: "First holder of the Henry Higgins Scholarship in Ireland; studied for three years in Paris; swears by ——, who taught her."

That dash signifies a deliberate omission on my part. My mother's teacher was a Cubist, a friend of Modigliani. He had arrived in Paris at the turn of the century. As the mark above shows, he has no name in this piece. He will turn up later here in a strange guise, but perhaps not a discreditable one. Nevertheless, he should remain nameless. It is part of my subject that the dissolution of his name here belongs to its intrusion elsewhere.

She studied with him, as the press cutting says, for three years. He was considerably older. She was beautiful, in her middle twenties, astray in the world. He was a good teacher. Her palette cleared. Her subjects were fresher. Her style was quicker. But with all the effect of his teaching, he failed to persuade her of one thing. She never became Cubist. She never showed any interest in that fractious, sweet-natured way of reassembling reality. Her heroes were Morisot and Bonnard. Her subjects were objects at the edge of elegy: quick impressions clarified by color but not exempted from it.

My mother hardly ever spoke to me about her painting. We did not talk about aesthetics, or ethics. We had a common bond; not a common language. I did not know how to describe to her the clear view her life gave me—of the past, of art, of Ireland. My rhetoric would have made her uncomfortable. We never talked about influence or authority. In the literary tradition of Ireland I felt restive and often disaffected. I got no such feeling from her. She never talked about those things. Now I wish she had. I wish we had.

But for all that, the question returns: Why include this subject here, at the threshold of my accounts of poetry and women? Some of the answer to that question is contained in another story which I include here, but in a shortened form:

My mother loved Berthe Morisot's painting. This in turn made me look more closely at Morisot's life. In the late spring of 1870, Morisot finished a painting for the Salon. Her position among the Impressionists had yet to be solidified. She was still striving for her place in the art world. This was her first submission. She called it *Portrait of the Artist's Mother and Sister*. Her letters show that she worked hard at it. She painted diligently to manage the formal setting. It was not easy. "My work is going badly . . . It is always the same story. I don't know where to start," she wrote to her sister Edma in 1875.

Nevertheless, she finished this painting. It is a studied portrait. It collects surfaces and figures: a lemon-wood table, a small vase of flowers. In the mirror the shapeliness of drawn-wide and bound-back curtains can be seen at the further end of the room. Two women are on the sofa. The younger is Morisot's newly married sister Edma. She is dressed in white, plainly pregnant. Her mother reads a book beside her.

A painting lives in space. The frame encloses it. But when the canvas is stretched and nailed, when the frame shuts around it, the life inside continues. I knew that from my mother.

In this case the frame could barely contain the painting. Pushing against those edges was the year, the circumstance, the drama. Paris stood at the edge of the Commune. In twelve weeks, the siege of the city by the Prussians would be established. "Would you believe, I'm getting used to the cannon's noise," wrote Berthe in September.

On the day it was to be submitted to the Salon, Edouard Manet, her friend and mentor, came to the Morisot house. The night before, he had said to Morisot, "Tomorrow after I send off my own painting I'll come see yours, and trust me: I'll tell you what you should do."

If this sounded ominous, it was. "The next day, which was yesterday," wrote Morisot in a letter, "he came about one o'clock, said it was fine, except the bottom of the dress; he took the brushes, added a few accents that looked quite good; my mother was in ecstasy. Then began my woes; once he had started, nothing could stop him."

Manet painted out large sections of Morisot's Salon portrait—"from the skirt to the bodice, from the bodice to the head, from the head to the background," as Morisot wrote. "He made a thousand jokes, laughed like a madman, gave me the palette, took it back again, and finally, by five in the evening, we had made the prettiest caricature possible. People were waiting to take it away; willy-nilly he made me put it on the stretcher and I remained dumbfounded."

When I was young, I struggled with authorship; with everything the word meant and failed to mean. Irish poetry was heavy with custom. Sometimes at night, when I tried to write, a ghost hand seemed to hold mine. Where could my life, my language fit in? "For the most part," wrote Nietzsche, "the original ones have also been the name-givers." But was this true? And how could I be original, if I couldn't even provide the name for my own life in poetry? At those moments of discouragement, there was a keen temptation to let that ghost hand do the work for me. I could have watched it as it moved fluently across that page, writing out the echoes. Somehow, I resisted that. All the same, I was aware of a shadow under the surface. Of a voice whispering to me: *Who is writing your poem?*

What moved over the canvas of Morisot's painting? What did she see unfolding in front of her as the splashes and pastels of Manet's brushwork corrected her own? A different vision? A higher authority? Those questions would come back: as hauntings, as shadows. When they did, I remembered too late that I had never answered them.

AS TIME WENT on, I found the shape of my life. I lived in a suburb in Dublin. I raised two small daughters. My husband Kevin and I filled the house with books, papers, children's things, our own writing.

It was a source of pleasure to me that the old city—deep in its past—was only four miles away. I imagined it the way I found it when I was fourteen, after a childhood in London and New York. On winter nights I thought of it as a familiar, unfolding from the lichen and black peat of the Dublin Hills all the way to the North Wall. I imagined its freezing rain and stone; the Liffey always flowing to the Irish Sea.

In light traffic, a twenty-minute drive took me into town. If I parked in the center of it I was in a web of streets which led up to College Green, and back down towards Stephen's Green. Which is where I was when I saw my mother's painting: the subject of this piece.

I was passing a small art gallery. I was on my way back to the car which I had parked at Trinity. The gallery was at a left-hand turn. Its street-facing walls were made of glass. The paintings inside were on show, some stacked against the wall, some hung on it. Shapes and colors making a carnival of a city corner.

Usually, I walked past. But that day a painting stopped me in my tracks: it was middle-sized, clearly visible through the plate-glass window, even in fading light. In the foreground of the canvas was a pair of gloves. Just behind them, in a green wash, was a vase. The light flowed in it, as if its physical surface were a transparency rather than a hindrance. In the vase were small flowers. Lily of the valley. They were my mother's favorite flowers. Their sweet, choking fragrance reminded me of cheap perfumes in London, bought for her on each of her birthdays, but never close to evoking the Paris streets of her youth. I thought of them, if I did, as the flowers of my childish failures.

I knew at once, without a second glance—without study, consideration, or hesitation—that it was my mother's painting. The colors were hers. The staging of the objects was hers. And so I went into the gallery and spoke to the man at the end of the long, narrow space. It was a perfunctory, quick exchange. I indicated nothing at all of my interest. The price was enormous. I asked quickly, again with a disguised casualness, about its provenance.

He announced the painter with an emphasis on the last syllable and with the gallery owner's disdain of the passing enquiry. My mother's teacher. I looked again to be sure. Yes, there was his signature, in the bottom right of the painting, where she usually put her own.

His signature. Her painting. Her vision. His price. And that was that.

I LEFT THE GALLERY and turned up towards Trinity. I had been a student there. I had read poems inside those rooms. I had written them there as well. I had worked in the old airy library above the front gate. I had even taught there as a junior lecturer of twenty-three. Now I walked up to College Green and looked back at the statues of Oliver Goldsmith and Edmund Burke which front the façade.

A poet and an orator. I knew something about them: chiefly, that they were eighteenth-century figures, born in a colony. That they had had no country. That they had a language, a rhetoric. Nothing more. The real nation had eluded them; not just their speech, but their imagination. It had flowed out beyond their shapely paragraphs and wistful cadences. They would speak of it and be spoken of by it. But they would never be its authors.

Suddenly I thought of an earlier time: of coming back to Ireland at fourteen. I had felt awkward. But I still sensed that I belonged somewhere: to the distaff side of Ireland. I was connected to it through my mother. Through her art, her anonymity, her origins in a small town marked on no map. Above all by the signs she made in oils on canvas.

Now that had changed. Standing there, I imagined the scene as it would be a few hours later—a summer darkness folding itself into the trees. Into the bronze ruffle on Goldsmith's jacket. Into the reflections on the windows of the gallery. Once I would have said to the statues, to quote Mary O'Malley's powerful line from her poem "St. John's Eve"— *Go back, I want to say, You are in the wrong place.* But not now. I could see that the statues had survived. They stood for a flawed authorship. But they had endured. But on the distaff side? What remained?

For this was the place where I had chosen to locate myself. In a place of shadows I called the past. I had thought about it; written about it. And at its gateway, and pointing to its interior, had always stood my mother. The mystery of her early life folded back and out into the flat lands and ordeals of an earlier Ireland. If I followed that silence, I was sure, I could enter it. Now what?

The truth looked at me coldly. That was her painting. Her authorship. She had assembled those flowers. She had constructed the complicated relationship between their petals and the background. She had worked on it, changed it, assembled it. No doubt she had changed it again. Then he had signed it. She had let him sign it. It was not the signature that shocked me; it was that consent. Down through the years, from a time when I had not even been born, came that faint *yes*.

I DROVE HOME. As I opened the door I could see, eye-level, some of my mother's paintings which we owned. But my mind was on only one of them, a few miles away. I thought of its presence there in the summer twilight. How the dark would reach that street and enclose the gallery.

And behind its doors, that painting. I thought of it lying against the wall: the small gleams of color, the fragmentary evidence of a young woman's life. I thought of those petals and their milky shine. How they would spread their oils and emblems—in that darkness and every one to come—above a false signature.

I asked myself a question. What did it matter that a woman I loved and a man I never knew had exchanged their claims, even their identities, for a brief moment? What did it matter that a young painter had let an older one—in a lost decade in a different country—write his name on her work?

It mattered. I was sure it did. That small canvas had a future as well as a present. That future—I believed this—was nothing less than my mind. Those greens, those imitations of air next to light, belonged to me. Those delicately colored arguments about the traffic between solid and space were tangled up with my sense of growth and survival. My mother's choice of shade and block was part of my first language. And now it seemed as if a man I never knew had signed my childhood.

But there was more. The shadow world in which I had taken up residence when I was a young poet was more complicated than I allowed. At that time, in that part of my youth, I called it the past. I gave it boundaries and called it by the name of my own country. Ireland. Then I re-named it again and called it my mother's life.

For all those acts of naming and re-naming, it was a complicated territory I was setting up house in. The rift between the past and history was real; but it was not simple. In those shadows, in that past, I was well aware that injustices and griefs had happened without any hope of the saving grace of elegy or expression—those things which an official history can count on. Silence was a condition of that past. I accepted it as a circumstance.

But only on certain terms. That the silences were not final. They were not to be forever. That they could be recognized; but also remedied. In my childhood they had been transformed at the end of my mother's day when she picked up an enameled mirror and turned her back to her own painting. Then, staring at a view which was over her right shoulder, she looked at her day's work. Considered it, judged it.

I saw her do this countless times. It would always be near dusk. Light would be leaving the room. When she looked in the mirror, she would have seen a day's worth of mistakes and some satisfactions as well. But as I watched her studying her own work—as I remembered it and reflected on it—it took on a different meaning. The angles, surfaces, compositions she achieved belonged to the craft of a few hours. But the act belonged to her lifetime. And mine.

I had depended on that act. It was the first sign of expressive power I saw as a child. The first article of feminine faith. Later I gave it a broad and glamorous interpretation. As I looked back I designated it as the moment when the hurts of an Irish past, of my mother's motherless life, of my own absence from anything familiar, healed into a little grace of remedy and articulation. A day had gone by. A million lights, refractions, rearrangements had taken place. Here on the canvas, and in the mirror, was a record of it all. But what was that record if, at the last moment, it was not presented as hers?

I remembered Virginia Woolf's bleak comment about the

improbability of a woman's authorship: "And undoubtedly, I thought, looking at the shelf where there are no plays by women, her work would have gone unsigned." The problem was my mother's work had been signed. But not by her.

A fuss about nothing? I could ask that question, but I couldn't accept it. For years I brooded about it. The doubts persisted. If anything, they grew. What did I feel had been violated by that long-ago moment? Nothing seemed clear. Whatever deference to hierarchy and authority had made her cede, even for a moment, the rights to her painting, was not what I believed I had inherited from her. The compliant student in Paris was not my obstinate, glowing mother who had opened an elusive past to me.

The mother I saw and understood was a figure of fable, thigh-deep in the mysteries and silences of the country she came from. I had studied that fable. I had learned that mystery. What she did in that studio in Paris was one thing. What I learned from her was another. The problem was I could no longer be sure how one had changed the other.

II

"The trade of authorship is a violent, and indestructible obsession," wrote George Sand. What is it we do when we sign a poem, a painting, a piece of writing? What is it we share when we let someone else do it? What on earth did I think had been changed in that room years ago?

Earth is the operative word. Whether I liked it or not, my life had been shaped by the fact that I came from one part of it. A small country. An island. A place where hundreds of years had passed without a trustworthy signature. The idea of an Ireland whose recent past—in historical terms—had been marred by false ownership had a meaning for me, as for so many others.

And yet, over time, I began to re-think George Sand's obsession. Not just in terms of Irishness. There came a moment when much of what I thought about poetry, language and even origin began to shift. I came to believe that how we see a painting, read a poem or write one can't simply be the outcome of a single fixed viewpoint.

It wasn't sudden or complete, this shift. It happened in increments, in gradual dawnings. The danger of describing it lies in the risk of giving it a coherence the process never had. I changed first. The poems I wrote changed later. Only after that did I add language and ideas. If all three seem to go together here, it's because retrospect flattens chronology. But one thing was clear from the start: Change depends on the questions we ask. Always providing we are willing to ask them. And at a certain point, I set out to find those questions.

When I looked at my mother's painting I had yielded to a small outrage. But what was its source? Was it based on a version of authorship? More likely, I thought, on a version of myself. A vast series of impressions goes into the making of any young poet. When I looked back at the night-time libraries, the wooden tables, the bookshelves I consulted, I could see myself sitting there, with a page turned. I could see, above all, that I was trying to be the author of myself.

But there was no escaping a predetermined narrowness. And no escaping that I learned to be a writer in the shadow of constraining influences. Young as I was, and Irish as I was, I still took most of my ideas from nineteenth-century British Romanticism. These were the texts I read in my convent school, which had found their way into every anthology and were then set in stone by college courses. I sat for hours on winter evenings, learning about the fever of this poet and the revelations of that one. I entered my reading the way an echo enters a sound. In the process, I never questioned that originality was a primary value.

Yet somewhere beyond those lamps, tables and pages was a vast and rich world of collaborative forms. A world in which originality was an almost meaningless concept. The ghazals, harvest songs, bardic schools, communal ballads were all there; all waiting. And all invisible to me. I had one template, and one only: the glamour and hubris of the individual poet. "The romantic image of the poet as a vulnerable personage in a hostile universe has not gone out of currency," writes David Lehman. I traded that currency.

At the start, therefore, the notion that poet and audience could blend their purposes, could co-author a poem from deep within a shared communal reality was foreign to me. Above all, the idea that a signature on a painting might be the last sign of an artistic mentorship rather than the first claim on a work of art never crossed my mind. A shadow land of artistic invention where the teacher and the taught, the poet and the listener, the creator and the created object could have fluid boundaries was still closed to me.

This book is about a journey. A journey with two maps. It recognizes my early ignorance of the vast distances of the poetic past—a horizon reaching far beyond my first sense of it; whose line nevertheless shaped my first map. It is about the dangers and glories of that first set of directions, which seemed to promise a young poet pride of language and exemption from ordinary life. It is also about the growing need for a second map. Another set of guidances in which my own individual voice could be heard. Where, the poetic past became something I could participate in, could even change, rather than having it determine my future. It is about making this second map and keeping it ready, while holding on obstinately—and even against advice—to the first. It is, above all, about reading and writing poetry with those two maps—which of course are figures for different or oppositional views—always available.

And yet the truth is, I started with one map. I had no idea there could be any other. That first map opened to me on teenage afternoons. On quiet midnights repeating and memorizing poems. Most young poets start out with a reverence for a past defined for them by someone else. Here are the great poems, they are told; these are the exemplars to learn from. A powerful set of suggestions does more than outline a literature. It confirms the young poet in their quest to join it.

For a long time I wanted nothing else. Besides, in those years I thought of myself as merely concerned with writing poems. I applied myself to the craft of a stanza, or to learning a more agile syntax. But the self-limitation failed. I would come to understand there is no poem separable from its source. I began to see that poems are not just an individual florescence. They are also a vast root system growing down into ideas and understandings. Almost unbidden, they tap into the history and evolution of art and language. They seek out their own progenitors. "The form of my poem rises out of a past," wrote Hart Crane. But which one?

I did not ask. At least, not at first. In the beginning, I merely wanted to introduce myself, hopefully and politely, to a single past: the one that awed me. I read continuously. I was sure if I kept reading I would find my name and my life as I looked behind me. And, because of that, I believed in the future. If I could bring together my life and my poems, I was certain I could go there. Despite the fact that by nationality and gender I was likely to be on the margins of the English canon, nevertheless I refused to feel excluded from its questions—its big, fearless questions. "I ask what is meant by the word Poet? What is a Poet?" wrote Wordsworth.

And so I settled: with one map, with one hope. The corner of a table under a cowled lamp in a library was where I most often found myself. When I went home I wrote poems at a smaller table. And this solitary, self-consciously questing life as a student was just near enough to the lives of poets I was reading—at least in my mind—to make me feel like them. The small proximity made me believe their power and independence could be my own. It was, of course, a false affinity. I was about to find that being a poet is more tangled in circumstance and accident than I would have believed.

"Poets have always known," wrote Muriel Rukeyser, "that one's education has no edges, has no end." At first, the expanding edges of my education looked decidedly everyday. I married. I moved house. I left the literary and confirming center of Dublin and went to live in a new suburb. Suddenly—every parent will understand the word—I had two young daughters. All at once, the library and the table and the friendly helmets of light became a memory. My working day as a poet now happened in the light and shadow of domestic arrangements. The thick notebook I wrote in could be lost and found under newspapers or a child's coat. The glamour and conviction of my first ideas of poetry—the feeling that I could emulate what I admired—began to be tested.

There was something painful about all this. I knew my world had changed. But the change was not clarifying. I loved the sensory world of neighborly routine and small children. The first delicate smell of an Irish spring; which was like crisp linen. Or the fragrance of peat fires in autumn. But inwardly everything was clouded with doubts. I could no longer pretend I was close to the poets I read. I was now at a distance from them; and the distance was growing. I still read my poetry books. I still wrote in my notebook. But I turned the pages now with hands which had come from lifting a child or shutting the back door against a gust of rain. How could I continue to make a text when I had lost a context?

The questions multiplied. Was there, I asked myself, anything of my old free life as a student-poet—anything of all its reading and searching—which remained? Could I even find myself as a poet in my new life? Or had I been an impostor in my old one? In reading the poets of a Romantic past had I learned—laboriously and with a fitful sense of grandiosity—all the wrong things: to invent myself for a world which would not have accepted me, and which could never, in any case, occur again?

It's almost impossible to re-construct an inner world. I lived a practical day-to-day life as a mother and wife. In my poems, I could echo Sharon Olds's eloquent words about wanting to "make a small embodiment of ordinary life, from a daughter's, wife's, mother's point of view." If I look back, I could accurately render the sloping road of the school run, the sycamore at the top of the hill. I could even summon the lost hum of the milk cart. Those are real, actual, describable. But the shadowy questions I lived with are harder to recover.

And so I will try to create a tableau here: a small stage-set of an inner world. A place where ideas of authorship occurred in an atmosphere as vivid as any view I saw outside my window. If I were to describe it accurately, it would be a silent mime. But for the sake of this argument, I will give it words. There are hazards in this. It means I have to create an artifice to replicate the way I built my thoughts: as though they happened in sequence, which they didn't. Nevertheless, this seems the only available method: the only way of getting at the subjective mystery: how one poet is made, and how an aesthetic grows in silence and doubt.

"Clearly the mind is always altering its focus," wrote Virginia Woolf in *A Room of One's Own*. Certainly mine was now changed. I had a new life. And yet after a while, for all my doubts and worries, I could see something had indeed survived from the old one. It was there when I went to the back room, late at night, and read a poem; or tried to write one. It appeared in front of me, unchanged and confirming.

What was it? It was that shining *I*. That obdurate and central witness of the poet. That first-person pronoun which signaled my hopes of becoming a poet. It was there when I went upstairs and took down a book, ready to be found in an image or a cadence. It was there when I opened my own notebook and wrote the first-person pronoun at the start of a line. Written or read, it could still provide me with a lightning-spark. It could still connect the tentative, half-formed entity which was all I yet could lay claim to and the beckoning hope of an achieved poetic self.

But there was a problem. If it was changeless—this pronoun and everything it promised—I was not. I opened a book of poetry now with different expectations. At times I grew restless with that old, glamorous part of speech—that relentless sign of the poet's singular domain. I wanted to see my new life in the old art. I wanted some recognition of the kettle I had just boiled, the sound of rain in the garden—and that they had come with me to the poem. I wanted to see their shadow. When I couldn't I wondered what reality this signal of the poetic self was refusing to encompass. And as I thought about this, I found that another word—an older one—crept out of the pages of poems I was reading. It shifted, shimmered, dissolved, re-formed and changed again. Not *I* any longer, but *we*.

Of course it had always been there. I had just not looked for it. Now that I did it seemed to be everywhere. Suddenly I was aware of its reach and brightness; of its application to my life. It recalled James Merrill's remark about Rilke: "He never says 'I' but in the *Duino Elegies* he seems to invite his readers into a community of shared suffering, or shared sensitivity. I couldn't wait to accept the invitation. I loved the feeling I got from those first-person plurals, as if one were being consoled and elevated at the same time."

It was a flexible instrument, this new pronoun. It was also inclusive of older histories, older communities. It could be the *we* of the balladeer, recording an event for which I was no longer the audience. Or the *we* of the Middle Ages poet, glued to other words by faith and authority. It might become the *we* of the Renaissance. Then, a few poems on, it might spin around and appear as the *we* of the Irish nation in the poems of Speranza in 1848; or, in another swift turn, manifest itself as a 1930s political poem.

For all its instability, its tendency to vanish in historic change, this new word—this *we*—commended itself. It seemed to include more of my life at that precise moment than the previous *I*. It gathered in the ordinariness of the house, the cheer and heat of the kitchen, the untidiness of the garden. As it did, it gave them a new shape. It spoke to me of down-to-earth communities which had once needed a voice. As mine did now. The time would come when this pronoun too seemed open to criticism, when the world it implied seemed another form of constraint. But for now I was drawn to it.

I have no doubt, even as I write them, that these are small revelations. And, certainly, they took place in small circumstances. But I promised a stage-set of a mind in process here; a picture of an evolving poet. If these pronouns seem not to provide that, then I have misrepresented them. The truth is, they were critical signs. Within the poem, they marked a vast difference from each other. Outside it, they signaled a growing tension in me. They pointed to alternate histories: towards opposite views of authorship. They were fractional as words; yet as symbols of composition they had enormous meaning. Within their difference I detected shadows of my own choices and dilemmas, and yet saw no hint of how to resolve them.

And so I have to re-imagine myself, back in those days when I was trying to find my own language. I have to remember late-night reading and an open book. And how I hesitated on one page over the silvery *I* of the poetic singular. And then turned back to the hallowed *we* of something older.

In the first instance, I could be upstairs on a winter evening, the curtains drawn, the garden seething with rain. Maybe I was reading *Frost at Midnight* or the tenth book of *The Prelude*, marveling at the way a single poet could stand against storm-forces of history, and be perfectly outlined. Or I could be looking at *The Buried Life* and be moved and persuaded by Arnold's sense of private revelation; of a "true, original course."

And yet the following week I could find myself—the rain turned to sleet, the children fretful and awake—changing my mind. Suddenly I would find myself agreeing with Robert Hass's comment, in his essay on Rilke in *Twentieth Century Pleasures* where he commented on the "sudden, restless revulsion from the whole tradition of nineteenth and early twentieth century poetry, or maybe from lyric poetry as such, because it seemed, finally, to have only one subject, the self, and the self—which is not life."

Then I too would become restless. I would open *Everyman* or *Pearl*, ready for the light and intensity of an earlier, more communal imagination. I would read the lines. I would see for myself how a community had co-authored the refrain of a ballad or the shape of a narrative. And so it went on. And so I continued, book by book. Back and forth.

But what exactly was at stake? To answer that, I have to insist again that I am describing a mime here. I was a poet hardly aware of the choices I was making, and yet knowing I had to make them. On a night of learning to read, of trying to write, I was looking for the micro-history of poetry. And yet it was there in front of me, closed into two pronouns.

And certainly, once inside the poem, two apparently tiny parts of speech assumed a larger role. They reached up from the pages of my books, these pronouns, crying out their different histories like street-hawkers. In the first-person singular I saw the glamour of the most enticing myths of composition. *Come with me*, it seemed to say. It beckoned me to the silhouette of the hero and the strength of soliloquy. Before I could respond, the *we* interposed itself. In its strength and poise I recognized the old dignity of poetry—its relation to the tribe. Different traditions, different directions. I was hopelessly torn.

And here I could leave it, this story. As a personal narrative; as a chronicle of reading and writing. As an unremarkable account of choices and changes of heart. I could abandon this account, fixed and printed as it is with the image of an indecisive reader and unconvinced poet; a woman shifting here and there between ideas of art and systems of authorship.

I could leave it were it not for one thing: The story changed.

There came a cumulative moment which extended and altered it. An inward sequence of dissents; a growing melody of constraint and skepticism. Finally—still upstairs, still with my books and my children and the sounds of a household—there came into my mind a plainspoken question: *Why choose?*

One question. And yet from that simple interrogation came a whole outworks of reason and light. Overdue as it was, it upended my thinking. Looking back, I could see things I had missed. How, for instance, almost from the start, my sense of being a poet had been shadowed by false alternatives. Far as I was from the center, deep as I was in a national rather than an international culture, I had felt a pressure to choose: Between the formal stanza and the open one. Between the canon and the tradition. Between modernism and what went before. Between the public poem and the private one. And finally, between two pronouns on a page.

It hardly mattered that the pressure was my own; was an internalized series of figments. The fact was I seemed to have started out as a poet in a world of deliberately crafted division: where modernism chastened indiscipline, and traditionalism scolded modernism. Where poetry fled from the back parlor and the evening recitation; yet no one could quite say where its home was now. Where two parts of speech strained to hold up different worlds.

WHY CHOOSE? Sometimes I imagine myself walking back into a Dublin twilight. Putting off the years. Shedding office buildings, computers, texting and traveling and the sorrows of aging. In my imagination, I stop on the same corner. By the illogicality and power of memory, the gallery is still there. My mother's painting is there.

And I am the same and not the same. I have had time to practice that refusal to choose. I have grown more comfortable with opposition; even with contradiction. I see more clearly now what I missed then. The elaborations of authorship, for instance. I realize that the *I* and the *we*—and everything they implied—were present even then in a way I failed to notice.

But what I mainly failed to see was my own limited understanding of making, and of being made. The situation unfolded a treasure of complications I never understood at the time: the painting itself was made by one person, signed by another and seen by a third; who was herself authored by the first. It existed in a nation which added another element, so that history was woven into the image and my reaction to it. In the end, the laying down of these different authorial layers infinitely complicated the idea of single authorship. So much so, that the idea on its own seemed no longer tenable.

None of these realizations solved the problem of the painting: its provenance remained disturbing and puzzling. In later years I would go back and forth about it. Had it simply been an afternoon's painting, done by the apprentice, but guided by the master and so signed by him? Hadn't my mother once pointedly told me what the strict definition of a masterpiece was? Not a defining work, she said, but the apprentice's final piece before being admitted to the guild? The questions continued; the answers never fit. But they showed me, those questions, that the issues raised were too rich and complex to be confined by a fixed viewpoint. It was not a moment to confuse authorship with ownership. And yet that was exactly what I had done.

The past does not change. But I had changed. If I stood again in the summer twilight, on that street, some things would be different. The angle of vision, to start with. The first time I saw the painting I looked at its signature, nothing else. I chose to see only what offended my early belief—that the single artist was the source of art. I allowed the definition of the author to overwhelm the existence of the art.

This time, if I could go back, I would consider both. I would look at the painting: the light wash of green, the quickly brushed petals. This time I would see that the signature and the image were more than just challenges to faith in a single aesthetic. They were separate fields of meaning—rich and problematic and inviting of new perspectives. Above all, their co-existence, even as contradiction, was not only possible but desirable. If art—and indeed poetry—was shaped by the interplay between individual and communal, then here was a chance to look into the fire of those contradictions, as if into a moment of origin. And so the question returns, *Why choose?*

And from that question comes the argument of this book. And its advocacy: That we can, and should draw two maps for the right and difficult art of poetry. That we can and should entertain even conflicted ideas to find a path through contradiction. That we can hold in poise oppositional concepts—I have put them forward here as *I* and *we*, as just one version of a possible opposition, but there are many others—without needing to erase one with the other. That we can take apparently opposed views of the history and practice of this art, and hold them reflectively in our hands as if they were two maps. And yet, in the end, come safely to a single destination.

The Rooms of
Other Women Poets

I

Iwas the fifth child of larger-than-life and wilful parents. I was born in Ireland and even now my parents seem to me perfectly Irish, completely of their time and place. They were eloquent and expressive. They waved their friends off after a late-night party, standing in doorways, framed by noise and laughter, blue cigarette smoke, whiskey kisses. Their life seemed to have happened in their words, before it ever got to their actions. I was their last child.

My father was first a civil servant, then a diplomat. But he thought of himself as the first, as if the second could only be a weak version of the civil servant's reach in a small country: the negotiations for coal, the granting of papers. It was the secret, hidden world of power which attracted him, not the flamboyant one.

My childhood was nomadic. We moved when I was young,

from Dublin to London, from London to New York. My father changed like a landscape. Never exactly handsome, but always high-colored in the face, his voice wounded by an old childhood stammer, he was almost always to be feared and listened to.

During those years, my relationship with my parents shifted. It was made up of distances, of empty rooms, of knowing they would be back next week or the week after. It was learning to do my lessons by myself, keep my thoughts to myself.

Like all children who are insignificant in a family—the last, the latest, the overlooked—I dreamed of having some surprising importance. But I was not quick at school and there were too many absences around me for me to prove myself to anyone. But even as a child, I felt restless, uneasy, put-upon by this life in strange cities with hard-to-get-at parents.

As I got older I read in random, undirected ways. I liked short poems, pithy stories and, above all, preposterous tales of girlish heroism. I sat up late at night staring at pictures in a Victorian encyclopedia. They were monochrome with a sickly yellow tint at the edge. They were of girls who had saved their town, or defied high water, or endured ordeals or were composed into perfection by virtues I knew even then I did not have and would never have. Patience, for instance. Silence.

I remember that one of them was called Grace Darling. She had saved lives. She had defied weather. The captions to the pictures said that she had gone out in a boat on high seas in some nineteenth-century storm under clouded-over stars. Even her name was a mixture of physical attributes and adoring attention. I envied her. I spent long evenings, in rooms I was uneasy in, in a home where I was anything but a heroine, practicing some sort of escape, some sort of immature empathy, looking at the old Victorian book.

What did they mean, those heroines? It was not that they offered any kind of intellectual life. In fact the opposite. Nevertheless, they had gathered around them, and had been the subject of, admirations, attentions, grainy colors and a painter's or photographer's skill. I wanted to be like them. To be that image, that shiny surface of grays and yellows and blacks that fell open in a book opened by some other young girl. Even though I knew it was impossible.

In fact I was at the outermost and final edges of possibility. In those years of the fifties, in London and New York, I lived, without knowing it, in a time when the profoundest changes were happening: when a radical alteration was getting ready to happen in the way a society saw young girls. And, as a consequence, in the way they saw themselves. I know now, as I knew then in some unclear way, that the loneliness of seeking out those strange girls in old books, with their hair blown back by sea gales, or their shiny paper skin cleared by thoughts of sacrifice, was a loneliness that went beyond me. It was deep in a society which needed to see itself in that skin, that expression. That had needed for hundreds and hundreds of years to offset unease with simplification.

I did not understand those changes. I was not meant to. Coming from a small country, with an intense Catholic idiom, my own language of girlhood was afflicted, was seized-up. Despite my intense awareness of my body, despite my feeling that it was yet another part of me that was displaced, I had no analytical understanding whatsoever. If I had some faraway sense that girlhood was the veiled mirror of a society, a place where it looked to recover its spoiled purity, where it was alternately cruel and grasping in the search for that purity, I could never have articulated it.

And so up in my room, opening the heavy burgundy covers of the encyclopedia, bending over and peering at those girls— immune as I believed them to be from my small humiliations and exclusions—I was the last figment of an old world. The hidden and unadmitted sexuality of my own culture would disappear, or so it seemed, almost overnight. In me it lay some- where between the mind and the body, a lost soul at that point waiting for a definition. That definition would come, swiftly and fiercely. Centuries would extinguish themselves and give out and give up their interpretations of girlhood somewhere between my last boyfriend and my first child. Everywhere, the old-fashioned superstitions would vanish. An entire civi- lization of crinolines and wasp-waists, of false conversations and choked-back desires, of late-night dreams and short-step dances, of rouge and flattery and simpers and flirtations, was about to disappear. And with it an empire of rude awaken- ings. But there in my room, at the gates of puberty, I knew nothing about this.

My childhood was ending. I came back to Dublin from New York at fourteen years of age, landed there like some mythical traveler on a magic island without maps or signals. I spent the week at boarding school. On weekends I went in with friends to O'Connell Street and ate in strange-seeming cafes where the food had Italian names but the sausages were plainly Irish. Then back out on the coast road, by train or bus, to boarding school. I was discovering poetry and books. If I was beginning to discover my own sexuality it was still too sunk beneath the reticence and rhetoric of my time and place.

In fact I was a foggy, erratic teenager: a fifth child, the

last in the queue for conversation or attention. Yet I knew, I always knew—like a consciousness of an overcast day—that I had a clever and wilful father. It was nothing I could have analyzed. And yet it was impossible not to register that we stood at extreme ends in our family, rigidly positioned there like statuettes: I, the latecomer, the youngest, the fourth girl out of five children. And he, the supremely important and attended-to presence.

There was very little that was sentimental or demonstrative about our relationship. He was a pious father. I was not a confiding daughter. But very early on, in my teenage years, I began to see a measurement and color to his conversation that was different to anyone else's. He knew how to speak. He knew how to address a single listener as if there was something at stake, as if the conversation was more than gossip or anecdote.

He lived in a dramatic world, sometimes a melodramatic one. Of late-night phone calls and hurried conferences. His conversation, his speech was mostly reserved for the people in those worlds. But sometimes in New York, on an occasional holiday when I visited from boarding school, he would speak to me across his desk in the room where he worked. It would always seem to me that I was there because the other children were grown. I had his attention by default.

At those times, almost as if I was not present, he would open a book and talk about when he had first read it. Or he would remember a thunderstorm in Ireland when he was a boy. How the lightning had cracked on the roof of their house in Bray, cracked over the Irish Sea and lit up the low line of Howth. How he had been a boy of seven, frightened in the storm, but had still crossed the length of it to comfort his younger brother. How in the morning, on the breakfast table, a small pile of copper pennies had been left there by his father. A reward.

I sat opposite him and listened. At those times, in some strange way, it was as if my skin was made of stone and my eyes were a vacant space. I was not ready to listen to him. I was not even clear why he was speaking to me.

Suddenly I was seventeen, the long years of childhood behind me. It was a warm, clear summer and I was working in a hotel before going to Trinity. I was out of boarding school. The harshly structured days were gone. I was free to look around. I had a summer job. I took the bus to work. I took it home again. After a while I noticed that whatever time of the day it was, they were there too: The iron fathers of the city. Grattan. O'Connell. Parnell. Huge statues, draped in bronze, with ore-colored hands. Standing over their statements, their promises. Looking up at them every morning, I felt like what I was, what I would always be: a daughter.

Then one more year. And at last I was a university student, eighteen years of age. I lived away from home, a short distance from my parents' house. Because I could walk home— Dublin was still eerily safe—I could stay past the last bus, into the small hours. Often my parents were out late and came in, and then the conversation began at midnight. More often than not, I sat in my father's study. Perched on a tiny, awkward trio of steps that went down into the room. It was a small room with high, falsely mullioned windows. The bookshelves behind my father's desk were narrow and steep and full of books on economics and history, on declarations of war and the public testaments of those who fought or prevented them. Outside was a curved tarmacadam drive and a road that led into the city, into the Dublin he had known and I was just beginning to know. Into the trees of the city, its poplars and willows and sycamores. Into its songs, canal waterways, malice and memories. Into the roads that were bricked, cobbled, surfaced, smoothed over. On cold nights, with the clear frosty air outside, I could almost follow those roads in my mind back into the meeting points and intersections that came together and drew apart and kept moving towards the river. Towards the statues: a crisp skin growing now over the outstretched hands, their icy lips still full of rhetoric.

My mother went to bed. As she left the room, there was always something small and unexpressed, as if I was losing her, as if I was losing myself. She was older now, the line above her eye drawn with less effect, the emblem she was to me much less clear than when I was younger. She did not talk in that high-stakes, clear way my father did. Her talk was more hesitant, more anecdotal. She left. I remained.

My father and I went on talking. One o'clock. Two o'clock. The conversations went in the way they must have done between fathers and daughters for centuries: What he knew. What I did not. What I might learn but could never really use. The depth of seas, the purpose of wars, the events that led to the French Revolution, the sound of gunfire on the Dublin streets in 1920. It was a gorgeous, packed world of facts, figures, histories. I listened. And listened. Did I ever think, once, that not a single fact there was one I knew I could use?

But I was clearer about myself. Or so it seemed to me in those early hours of the morning. A teenager's body, that site of pain and doubt, seemed to be polished away, turned into a mist of syntax and power as I talked. Back in my flat the lipstick, the compact with its pale powder, for flattening the color of skin, still waited for me. And the mirror and my new eyeshadow. But for now, for a few hours of peace, I could disown them. And still the facts, the figures, the shapely histories, the kings, the foreign wars, the famous speeches kept arriving. And I could be part of them, I could be privy to them, I could be sexless, I could be powerful, if . . . If what? What was it I lacked?

Sitting there on the step listening, trying to nod my comprehension, joining in where I could, was the nearest I had ever come to the flatteries and glamourings of the self I imagined and yearned for in childhood. Those girls in my encyclopedia, dashed by the storm, drawn in sharp inks, were different. They were chosen. Here for a while I was different—plucked by words out of the routines and rituals of young womanhood. Suddenly made complicit in battles and speeches, in the collection of an army in snow-bound Moscow, in a last desperate speech to the Irish Parliament, in the elegy for the Athenian dead.

Book after book was pulled down from the tightly packed shelves. I was shown the titles, told about the authors, invited to listen. More than that, I was being allowed to eavesdrop on great decisions, treated as if I could share their source and their outcome. In a serious, unexpected way I was being encouraged to admire those centers of the earth, of civilization, of culture which had made me. *But was it,* a small voice kept asking at the back of my head, *me they had made? Or my father?* And then the voice would prompt—*But could it be you?*

I remember the hidden seasons outside the small windows. The way the frost made harsh margins on the leaded sections. How the daffodils edged the driveway in spring. How the summer nights were full of stirrings, fidgetings, as if not a single bird or leaf or inch of wind was ready to settle into silence.

The conversations were brilliant and symmetrical on my father's side. They represented not simply a view of the world, but also a view of what was important in it. I sat there on the steps, my knees hunched up, my chin in my hand, listening. And listening. There in that small room, at the edge of that city with its metal and marble orators, a procession of those significances went by. A book would be taken down, a short speech would be read out, or a long one. Grattan to the Irish Parliament. *I found Ireland on her knees. I have watched over her with a paternal solicitude.* Or Pericles to the Spartan dead. Or Napoleon leaving an ice-bound Moscow. Just occasionally a small detail appeared, like a stowaway on a boat: that his grandmother had come from the Comeragh Mountains. That she had had to walk six miles every day for water. Six miles there. Six miles back.

And then for a moment I would look up, as if someone had called my name from a distance. His grandmother. Walking the hills above Clonmel. That steep, brackish rise of the Comeraghs with its wild broom and hawthorn. Its rough terrain and coarse outline. She had walked there, setting out for water, bringing it back, heavy and necessary. My great-grandmother, knowing nothing about battles and orations. But nothing also about swaying dresses and flirtation and pretence. Just for a moment, in those sentences, I saw something of myself. A narrative I might enter.

But then history would come back: well attired, speaking in sonorous tones. My name would fade. No one, after all, had called me. And the night and the moon would fade too. Sometimes, on summer mornings, the light would inch into the sky at 4 a.m. My father would stand up, ready to go, with a fond good night. I would get up and let him go past. And then look around the small room—a few books out on the desk, the ice cubes almost melted in the bucket. I was trying to frame some thought, some clear impression. Where in everything I had heard, in every territory we had covered, was one inch where I could breathe or live?

And yet there was nothing simple about it. It was never clear-cut. For those moments when my father turned and talked to me it was as if some old dream was being prodded into life, even as a new one was put at risk. Those legendary girls, the water dashed on their clothes, their hair streaming in black-and-white paintings, what after all had made them heroines? This. This very thing. This onset of attention, and powerful talk and arcane knowledge. They had not been— of course I knew it by now—heroines in and of themselves. They had been made heroines. They had been allowed to be heroines.

For so many women there must be one place where the dream of becoming a poet died. There, in one spot, she— whoever she was, whenever she lived—let go of that hope. One house, perhaps. One room. One set of walls, one aspect she can still see when she closes her eyes and thinks bitterly, or sadly about what she lost.

I did not give it up. But if I had I would have thought back to that place. A small room with steps down, on which I sat night after night in what seemed to be an informal posture. With a dark red carpet and a comfortable armchair and small windows. But which, of course, had more of the domestic updated version of sitting at a great man's feet than I would have ever realized or ever admitted. Where I, the youngest daughter of a clever, wilful and in some ways Victorian man, waited in vain for the big wings of wax.

II

In later years, when I remembered my conversations with my father, I thought of them as providing a theater: a contest between presence and resistance. I saw that small room as a site where the growth of poetic will was weighed in a delicate balance. Between power and submission. Between authority and independence.

When Adrienne Rich published "Split at the Root," her beautiful essay on Jewishness and inheritance, I was moved and guided by her honesty. "My father was an amateur musician, read poetry, adored encyclopedic knowledge," she wrote there. "He prowled and pounced over my school papers, insisting I use 'grown-up sources'; he criticized my poems for faulty technique and gave me books on rhyme and meter and form. His investment in my intellect and talent was egotistical, tyrannical, opinionated, and terribly wearing. He taught me, nevertheless, to believe in hard work, to mistrust easy inspiration, to write and rewrite; to feel that I *was* a person of the book, even though a woman; to take ideas seriously. He made me feel, at a very young age, the power of language and that I could share in it."

The power of language. I had felt it in that room. I had also felt an oppression and loneliness which clung to those words. As time went on, I grew curious. Had the same thing happened to other women poets? If so, I wanted to know. I wanted to see those lives. To find a woman in a room, late at night, a few stars stuck to the window. To witness again late night talk and unspoken resistance.

I thought back to those evenings, my chin in my hand, words failing me. Where had those failed words ended up? In images? In cadences? All I knew was I had resisted something. But what? Authority? Tradition? I knew that rejecting a body of wisdom could be seen as adolescent. But in memory, it felt like something more substantial: the fending off of the settled products of knowledge in favor of the small beginnings of self-knowledge.

In her book *Scaffolding* Jane Cooper weighs her own struggle to find an inward authority and wonders at her own hesitation. "Is this primarily a political story," she asks herself, "having to do with how hard it is for a woman to feel the freedom that would let her develop as a writer, even when she has it?"

The idea of a woman finding herself as a poet within an unlikely, stay-at-home resistance stayed with me. It had the feel of an intimate allegory. I began to see my silences in those conversations as revealing. Not so much a chapter in father-daughter relations, as the start of a connection between being and becoming a poet. The more I thought of it, the more it became an outline of inverse influence. A wilful detour from the usual narrative of poetic inheritance.

And yet poetic inheritance mattered. I knew it did. Poets manage their growth by opening their minds. They plunder personal circumstance or formal opportunity. "This then is a book! And there are more of them!" said Emily Dickinson after one of her first reading adventures. I remembered the silvery, falling-apart pages of my first anthology of poems. The obsessive turning backwards and forwards, looking for old language and new instruction.

So here I was with something of a double vision. With two maps. On the one hand, the realization that the poetic past is a necessary engine of authority. On the other, the knowledge that a poet's resistance to that authority can also be vital. What would I find if I joined those two ideas?

I found Elizabeth Barrett Browning. A troubling, compelling mix of independence and compliance. A poet linked to the tradition and yet in defiance of it. Above all, a writer and a woman whom—using one or the other map only—I might have overlooked. But now, holding firmly to both, someone I felt I could engage and understand.

She is not easy to understand. "Fate has not been kind to Mrs Browning," wrote Virginia Woolf. "Nobody reads her, nobody discusses her, nobody troubles to put her in her place." But I read her. And I wanted to put her in her place. I will start therefore by trying to make a collage, rather than just a collection of facts. Which means beginning with her appearance, as the age did. In her own words, she was "five feet one high . . . eyes of various colors as the sun shines."

But the sun rarely shines in the posed and stiff portraits we have of her. She wears navy-dark serge or wool dresses: hard to gather in the hand and yet beautifully stitched. The dress can stand in for all the reticences which are partly chosen in her life and partly habitual. It can be a sign of those mornings when visitors were not received. When she refused a friend's calling card. When she chose to lie in a room, the dark serge gathered around her.

But although the dress is a clue, it's not enough in itself. There must be other ways, to paraphrase Woolf, of putting her in her place. And so I add them in. To start with, a harsh backdrop of iron and mill sweat. And then the sound of trains and the sight of sailing ships. It may sound as if these things are irrelevant. But they are not. In this darkened room where the dress flows around itself, to which the visitor rarely penetrates, there are shadows. The shadows are not just those of poetry. They are also those of empire.

Mill dust and the clang of iron. The making of ships's hulls. The forging of space in which cotton and paper and steel can be produced. Those sounds fill a whole century. They are noisemakers in an era of change and expansion.

In the room of the so-called poetess these sounds matter. She cannot hear them, cannot identify them. But they were at her cradle. Empire has more to do with her seclusion than she will ever know. Empire, which has touched the merchant and the sailor and the politician, now touches the poet's life. Not just the life of the male poet; although it will do so in the cases of Tennyson and Arnold. But hers as well.

In fact, the poetess—and Elizabeth Barrett Browning almost inaugurated the category—lives in a world defined by empire. The trays which are taken to her room. The noiseless servants protecting her rest. The view from her window of acres which have never been re-distributed. These are fractions of it. She herself is another fraction. The role of the poetess should itself be seen as a primary fiction of empire. A strange alloy of the demands of power and the unease of an age.

This, unfortunately, is where everyone starts to lose patience. I can't agree with Germaine Greer's witty and dismissive comment In *Slip-Shod Sibyls: Recognition, Rejection and the Woman Poet*: "The more women adored poetry the less they were able to write it . . . It is less crucial for women to work out how men did this to women than it is to assess the extent to which women did it to themselves."

But I recognize the challenge she is making; and it deserves an answer. Unfortunately this phase of Elizabeth Barrett

Browning's life does not provide it. She seems merely to have internalized and personalized these power relations. "I am of those weak women who reverence strong men," she wrote in a letter to a friend.

Elizabeth Barrett Browning's first years were spent in the English countryside. She was born in 1806. By her twenties, the intensity and claustrophobia of her life were established. And mostly by her relationship with her father, Edward Moulton Barrett. He was a saturnine man. He had owned estates in Jamaica. He had made and lost money.

He was also darkly possessive. A proprietorial ownership was directed at all his children. But Elizabeth especially. When he refers to her in a letter as "a beloved invalid," the words have an ominous tilt. She was certainly frail. That much is clear. What is not clear is why her frailty evolved from circumstance into identity. And then from identity into a necessary condition. Nor is it clear why, when she fled his house at the age of forty—to marry Robert Browning—he never spoke to her again. "May your father indeed be able to love me a little," she wrote to Browning at that time, "for my father will never love me again."

In the anguish and enclosure of her relation with her father, Elizabeth Barrett Browning proves a point: All women poets have one thing in common. They are all daughters of fathers. Not simply daughters of a natural father, but also daughters within—and therefore sometimes entrapped by—the literature they seek to add to.

What does this mean to the woman who becomes a poet? It could mean, to begin with, an uncomfortable question. A question which must surely have occurred to Browning in the dusk of her room in Wimpole Street: Is it possible that the ordinary fate of being a daughter is changed, even subverted, by the extraordinary act of writing a poem? And how is a woman poet to live and think while she steals that fire?

I want to imagine more than personal circumstance around that question. Elizabeth Barrett Browning's solitude, her shrinking were not isolated events. In her time, poetry itself was retracting. A boisterous, robust craft had begun to inch off to the alcove and the ivory tower. An art which had been filled with vitality and ambition in the earlier part of the nineteenth century was starting to be thin-blooded and solitary. The old country of human accident and event was being abandoned. A new country was made called Imagination and poets were sent to live there.

In that sense, the woman who lived in this room—with her nervous avoidance and insistence on vocation—was a tenant of the sacred places in which the poem was now making its home. But she was only a tenant. Elizabeth Barrett Browning did not own an inch of the land. She had been designated a poetess. Inevitably, she was both elevated and sidelined by the categorization.

And so her headaches and darkened rooms seem especially emblematic of the reduced status of the poet. But for all that, when I read her, I still wanted to imagine that space. I furnished it with images of the rooms I had seen in childhood. I filled it with the conversations I had once had. I imagined an endless dialogue with her saturnine father: complete with anxious-to-please words and ready affirmations of his authority.

I returned to the letters. Her fear and love are plain there, painfully bound together. When she eloped with Robert Browning, Edward Barrett broke with her. He disinherited each of his children who married. She never saw him again.

Her first letter to a friend after her marriage describes the strange atmosphere she had lived in for all her young womanhood. Suddenly we are staring down into an underworld, the walls jeweled with her needs and nervousness, her sickness and his strength. "Never has he spoken a gentle word to me," she wrote, "or looked a kind look which has not made in me large results of gratitude, and throughout my illness the sound of his step on the stairs has had the power of quickening my pulse."

Elizabeth Barrett Browning, I am afraid, is merely a sidebar in this book. She deserves more space and a closer look. She is a figure of tense and fascinating contradictions. By allowing those contradictions to exist, neither banishing them with certainties nor shutting them down with conclusions, she began to exist for me too. She became too real to be disowned.

And the truth is I could have disowned her. Her submissiveness grated. Her rhetoric could seem forced. But for all that, she corrected and instructed my earliest reading. The Victorian ethos which produced the heroines and storms I once pored over produced her as well. But she was real. They were fantasy.

Where there is heroism to be found, it is in her odd generosities. If she never contested empire, she nevertheless advocated freedom for Italy. If she never disowned the ugly relation with her father, she spoke of him with such warmth and understanding at the end that it seemed to heal her old submissive relation with him into a kind of equality.

There is real courage also in the slow unbinding of the pieties which defined her early life. Her gradual taking possession of language and poetry. Her acceptance of a new husband and another country. Not everyone acknowledged her struggle. Virginia Woolf remained acerbic: "We all know how

Miss Barrett lay on her sofa; how she escaped from the dark house in Wimpole Street one September morning; how she met health and happiness, freedom, and Robert Browning in the church round the corner." It is plain that Elizabeth Barrett Browning did not meet Woolf's standard of proof.

But to me at least she proves a different point: the need for two maps. With just one, this poet would disappear into stereotype. With just one, she could easily become a series of sound bites: less canny than the Victorians, less skeptical than the Romantics. The second map would not work on its own either. It would make her a ghost in an age of modern women's poetry: a caricature of submission.

Put together however, they direct the reader to a fascinating writer. In the narrow compass of her life, Elizabeth Barrett Browning confronted large things. Whatever her lost conversations with her father contained, we can imagine them as true dramas of Victorian authority: framing an age and being framed by one. In her later work—in poems like "Mother and Poet"—she voiced a contest between the creative and the institutional. It is not hard to guess at the source. She represents alignments of identity and self-discovery that are well worth looking at. And yet the truth is, had I not used these two contradictory sets of directions to go back to her— seeking her out as a traditionalist while also recognizing her as radical and disruptive—I would have lost her.

Becoming an Irish Poet

I

When I was a student I could choose which way to go home. The front gate of Trinity brought me to College Green. The back gate to Nassau Street. On winter nights, I preferred the second way. There was less traffic. It took me down by Clare Street to Merrion Square. The streets would be quiet and empty then. The swan-necked streetlamps were on. The windows looked like stranded moonlit rectangles.

Merrion Square is one of the old treasures of Georgian Dublin. An ambiguous gift of colony. On the nights I walked down to it, it was eerie and silent. But a century earlier it would have been different. The whole neighborhood was then the center of Dublin professional life. I could easily summon it as I stood there in the dark. Haloed gaslight. Fashionable carriages over the cobbles. The rush and noise of a ruling class.

In the nineteenth century, this was the hub of a garrison

city. A place where doctors and lawyers plied a trade guaranteed by their fashionable clientele. The buildings are still lanky and imposing. The fanlights, then as now, spun off down the street, making a vista of semicircles. The topmost windows looked over chestnut trees. The demeanor of it all revealed a purpose. A deceptive grace closing its iron grip of class and dominion over an unreliable nation.

When I came to the edge of the square, I stopped. It was not a place I could or should have wanted to imagine. Far from it. My grandmother had died, a poor sea captain's wife, near there. She was just past thirty. She died in a fever ward, in the lying-in hospital at the end of the street. The generations of women from which she came—products of Boyne Valley townlands and small parishes—were more likely to have entered those houses to clean them than to be entertained.

And yet, as often as not, I stayed looking up. A house stood on the corner. One façade pointed at the trees of the square. Another looked towards Trinity. It was a tall structure, not quite rid—even in the present moment—of the hubris of its origins. But I was not looking up because of a bygone era. I was there for a previous tenant.

Her name was Jane Francesca Elgee. She was the grandaughter of a Church of Ireland archbishop. She would become far better known as the mother of Oscar Wilde. But in the tumultuous decade of the 1840s she was a young woman, still unmarried. She was writing poetry and trying to have it published. She had not yet read her legendary son's comment: "Others write the poetry that they dare not realise." For her, there would be no distance between poetry and self-realization.

A few snapshots from contemporary accounts tell the story. A glimpse of her in a drawing room here or there, being introduced or introducing herself, gives a sense of energy and self-importance. Here she is, handsome and insistent in a damp house in Leeson Street in 1846. She is telling the editor of *The Nation*—a fervent patriotic journal—that he must publish her poems.

Now she is in a Dublin courtroom in 1848. It is tense and crowded. This is the critical moment of another about-to-fail Irish rebellion. Jane Elgee is also at a turning point. She has become Speranza. Irish national poet and acting editor of *The Nation*. She sits in court, high-colored and excited.

The Nation is on trial because it has published an anonymous article called *"Jacta Alea Est"* (The Die Is Cast). It is a call to arms, an invitation to Irish insurrection. This is not something to be taken lightly. Charges of treason are in the air. Long prison terms and harsh transportations will soon follow show trials of the organizers of the 1848 rebellion. Under British law the article in *The Nation* amounts to sedition.

It is hard to recover an age. Its clothes, its transport, its voices. They fade obstinately away. What is left are ghosts of the time: gestures, events. But some features remain the same. Ireland was then, as later, a land of rhetoric and ritual. In Paul Muldoon's lines from "The Old Country": *Every resort was a last resort / with a harbour that harboured an old grudge. / Every sale was a selling short.*

And here, in that climate of rhetoric, was a seditious article. And the young woman who wrote it. Because she was, of course, the author. At that moment, she must have felt she was, in Natasha Trethewey's vivid phrase from her poem "South," in a *state that made a crime / of me.* Speranza's pride and involvement must also have been obvious to everyone in that courtroom. Her face flushed. Her mouth working. But the danger is irrelevant to her. The adventure is uppermost.

Finally, she stands up excitedly and claims authorship. She is ignored. Women are not plausibly considered for treason charges at that point in Irish history. But newspapers are: *The Nation* is shut down.

But before that the journal had published her poems. At first, under the male sobriquet of John Fanshawe. They had attracted immediate attention. "Our new contributor promises to rival Mangan in the melody and fullness of his phrases," says the editor. But the male pronoun did not fit Jane Francesca Elgee. She revealed her true identity and took the *nom de guerre* Speranza.

On those cold nights, on my way home, I almost always stopped at the house. The windows glowed out into an Ireland they could no longer beckon. I stood there, looking up. And so I stumbled unwittingly into one of the contradictions of being an Irish poet. To claim her poetic identity in Ireland in 1848 implied an unswerving devotion to nationhood by Speranza. Or at least the fiction of it. And in the making of that identity at that time, rhetoric was encouraged. Hyperbole was welcomed. The results are all too plain to see: Speranza's poems are not good. But no, that does not say it accurately. Speranza's poems are absolutely unconvincing.

And yet on those starry, frosty nights it was not her bad poetry I was thinking of. In fact the opposite. I was thinking about two lives—hers and mine. I had moved around as a child. I had lived in other cities. I had learned no dialect of belonging; I knew no idiom of attachment to place or its purpose. Now here was a woman who made no difference between words and purposes. "Once I had caught the national spirit," she wrote, "the literature of Irish songs and sufferings had an enthralling interest for me. Then it was that I discovered that I could write poetry."

How extraordinary that must have been, I said to myself, beating my hands together in the cold. To find a nation through your poems. To acquire your poems through a nation. Never to sense tension or division between them. To be guilty of sedition and yet certain of your own loyalties. To use your words to prove a place and know that proof would become an article of faith to others.

I had yet to understand the meaning of Mark Strand's powerful poem "The Idea" where the definition of origin is reached for and never fully grasped. It appears in his poem as a small, glowing house, stripped back to its Puritan worth and yet somehow inhospitable to visitors, even while being available to their understanding: *But that it was ours by not being ours / And should remain empty. That was the idea.*

On those cold nights, I still believed origin was simple and graspable. I was still convinced, after my own nomadic childhood, that coming to a cause and place which seemed to embody both was a rich source for a poet. And so when I looked up at Speranza's window, it was not her failures I was imagining. It was her happiness.

It would take years to see my mistake. To understand the difference between the place a poet claims and the place a poem renders. Speranza stated and re-stated her love for Ireland—in verse, in polemic, in pamphleteering. And yet Ireland—even her high-caste Anglo-Irish version of it—disappeared into her poems. She contributed thirty-nine poems to *The Nation*. They are almost all bellicose and patriotic. Her stance is never less than public and theatrical:

> *What! are there no MEN in your Fatherland,*
> *To confront the tyrant's stormy glare,*
> *With a scorn as deep as the wrongs ye bear,*

With defiance as fierce as the oaths they sware,
With vengeance as wild as the cries of despair,
That rise from your suffering Fatherland?

"Lyric cancels out time," wrote Richard Howard in a review of James Wright. It can also cancel out reality. Even so, the extent to which a nation—its complicated history and local suffering—is erased by these lines is sobering. In the nineteenth century the intellectual drift of the poet was usually subsumed in the artifice of a poem. We deduce the aesthetic will of a Tennyson, of a Dickinson, not from what they wrote but from the way they wrote it.

But in Speranza's case the subject consumes everything. Language, tone, syntax all vanish into national sentiment. There is no voice. "We fall back on that term, voice, for all its insufficiencies," writes Louise Glück in *Proofs & Theories*. "It suggests, at least, the sound of an authentic being." But there is no sign of that in Speranza. And none of that reticence implied in the comment by the eminent Irish poet Maire MacEntee about her own work: "In most of my poetry you can see that drawing back, bringing the poem right up to the crisis and pulling back."

Speranza never pulls back. She yields at every turn to the demands of her subject. Finally, it becomes hard not to look at this word-bath of acid, in which details and subtleties are dissolved, without feeling something like horror. This is an Irish political poet—and there were few women in the category—whose poetry is a vanishing act. Nothing is left but the flourish, the quick sweep of the empty cabinet, the self-congratulatory length of the wand.

What happened to Speranza? She was, after all, an accomplished, courageous woman. She was the mother of Oscar

Wilde. She lived through a turbulent part of Irish history and recorded it. Yet she emerges as a caricature.

The truth is, a national tradition is a wilful editor. I would later find it oppressive. But as a teenager I was both swept away and lost. I had come back to Ireland at fourteen years of age. I had studied Irish history. I had read speeches from the dock. I had tried to fuse the vivid past of my nation with the lost spaces of my childhood. I had learned the battles, the ballads, the defeats. It never occurred to me that eventually the power and insistence of a national tradition would offer me only a new way of not belonging.

"We are the products of editing rather than authorship," wrote George Wald. In that sense, Speranza was edited. Then again, the compression and reduction of her role, the limitations of her horizon, had been her choice. Through her, I first came to realize that a national agenda could be an editor. I was less aware it could also be a censor. And yet one of the most striking and historic poems in the Irish canon seemed to prove it. If not in the text, then clearly in the transmission of the text.

II

The year was 1773.

Eibhlín Ní Chonaill and Art O'Laoire were a young married couple. He had recently returned from a stint of service in the Hungarian Hussars. The image we have of him—more a snapshot than an image—is of a truculent Irish noble. We learn that he astonished the local people of Macroom by standing on a rolling barrel down the steep main street, with his sword— illegally according to the harsh British Penal Laws—still buckled on. "I foresaw," wrote one of his relatives, "that his violence and ungovernable temper would infallibly lead him into misfortune."

In that same year Art O'Laoire, already declared an outlaw, was struck down as he galloped across a townland called Carrigonirtane. He was twenty-eight years of age. A single musket shot killed him. His riderless horse trailed back without him. According to the poem she composed, Eibhlín Ní Chonaill caught the horse's bridle and rode to the place where her dead husband lay in the briars. Then, in the darkness, she dismounted and went to his lifeless body. She put her hand in his blood. She drank it. And all at once, one of the most celebrated and ambiguous moments of Irish literature is ushered in.

Eibhlín Ní Chonaill's poem, composed for her murdered husband, is an Irish-language lament, a spoken and stylized echo of elegy. A poem therefore composed in one of the oldest languages, and in a venerable form. She might have echoed the words of Nuala Ní Dhomhnaill, written in her fine essay "Why I Chose to Write in Irish: The Corpse That Sits Up and Talks Back": "If there is a level to our being that for want of any other word I might call 'soul' (and I believe there is), then for some reason that I can never understand, the language that my soul speaks, and the place it comes from, is Irish."

The soul and the place in this poem are obviously rooted in the Ireland of the eighteenth century and the language which was still at that time its psyche. But since I did not speak Irish, having been away as a child, my encounter with the poem was in English. There have been fine translations since, but I came across it first in Frank O'Connor's incantatory version: I still remember the musical, furious voice he provided Eibhlín Ní Chonaill with, and the way he had her describe, in his version, that single extraordinary gesture of lifting her husband's blood to her mouth: *I did not wipe it off / I drank it from my palms.*

A young woman. An expressive grief. But now—for the purposes of this argument—I need to swerve away from her. I need to eavesdrop on a lecture given almost two centuries later in 1966. It is Peter Levi's inaugural lecture as Professor of Poetry at Oxford. In the course of it, he describes *The Lament for Art O'Leary* as "the greatest poem written in these islands in the whole eighteenth century." A true accolade. And yet the statement, for all the power of its tribute, serves to erase the poem's identity. *The Lament for Art O'Leary* was not written. It was composed. The difference is critical.

How did this happen? I suspect the answer is simple: Peter Levi modeled the poem on examples of elegy he knew and understood. The real question his error poses is about which view of authorship—or which combination of views—allows us to return to a text and address the reality of a poem and its maker. Which one will allow us to discover the true identity of Eibhlín Ní Chonaill: this young woman not yet thirty, her hand dipped in her husband's blood, her lips composing an elegy that reaches far back into oral literature?

I'm able to attempt the question here because of the fine work of an Irish scholar and writer, Angela Bourke. The title of the poem in Irish is *Caoineadh Airt Uí Laoghaire*. The name suggests the origin. The poem is a keen—a subtle re-arrangment of the melodies and repetitions of the Irish *caoineadh*, or keen; an art of the dispossessed.

I never heard the keen. It was reduced to a legend when I was young; another emblem of an Ireland I could never catch up with, that had almost disappeared. But my father had seen and heard it. As a young man in Galway he watched the emigrant boat get ready to leave for England. A group of old women—these were the keeners—gathered on the pier. As the boat drew out the old women put their shawls over their heads and began the keen. My father remembered the sound as eerie and terrible.

Our first glimpse of Eibhlín Dubh Ní Chonaill is of a new woman using an old art. "We see a chasm opening at her feet," Angela Bourke writes, "a class divide which grew wider through the nineteenth century . . . On the one side of that divide stand orality, the Irish language and poverty; on the other are literacy, English and all the trappings of patriarchal and colonialist modernity. Eibhlín Ní Chonaill belonged to the class that became modern."

I was fascinated that this almost-modern woman, in her moment of loss, reached for an age-old and communal art form. A poem which is part a fresh-spoken grief and part an age-old formula. An elegy poised between worlds. A subtle and powerful negotiation with past laments. If we could only understand it, we might get a deeper insight into poems as far apart as the *Iliad* and *Gawain and the Green Knight*.

But the opposite might also happen. If we misread this poem, then we lose our one and only chance as readers to stand beside Eibhlín Ní Chonaill. And if we don't take up position there, we lose our opportunity to look into the age-old relation between the formulaic part of an art form and the extempore parts made up by its speaker.

Which is precisely what happened. Throughout the nineteenth century, in the light of new ideas of authorship, Eibhlín Dubh Ní Chonaill begins to disappear. *The Lament for Art O'Leary*, as it came to be known, is pushed, and turned, and re-made in the shape of other conventions. Its origins are obscured by contemporary interpretations, most of them British or Anglo-Irish. It is romanticized, glamorized, pulled out of shape. Its author, an Irish woman caught in a moment of historical change, is replaced by a simplified nineteenth-century heroine: a stereotype of Lady Morgan's Wild Irish Girl. Gradually the real woman, the flesh-and-blood aunt of Daniel O'Connell, the young and desperate widow in her late twenties who knew the old arts and availed of them in her grief, vanishes. How did this happen? Again, Angela Bourke provides the explanation:

> In the last years of the nineteenth century the question of Home Rule for Ireland was being hotly debated. Colonialist rhetoric was at its height in England, and those who opposed Home Rule habitually denigrated the Irish—along with Africans, Native Americans, and other colonized peoples—as brutish and ignorant. Nationalist scholars and the literati of the Irish revival were at pains to counter this propaganda, highlighting the aristocratic elements of the texts they edited, translated and adapted from mediaeval manuscripts and contemporary folklore. That *The Lament for Art O'Leary* could be read as a text of marital devotion among noble and high-minded Irish people was enough to guarantee it a place in the canon of Irish literature then being formed.

And so, piece by piece, a young woman disappears. A vital clue to our past and our poetry fades out. Like a figure cut out of a photograph, she becomes a missing space, replaced by more comfortable images. Her rich and tense relation with the keen-makers goes. Her historical balancing act goes. Above all, what her art can tell us about the deep connections between a communal archive and a single art—all that goes too.

And so for want of a wider view of authorship, a subtle Irish artist is transfigured into a one-dimensional Victorian heroine. The overwriting of her achievement by ambitious Irish and British canon-makers shows us something we need to keep in mind: that received ideas of authorship can suppress actual ones.

III

One question remained. If a national tradition could edit one woman poet and censor another, how could I myself survive it? I was eighteen when I stood looking up at Speranza's window. My laying out and unweaving of these national threads would come quickly over the next few years. My sense of a national tradition that needed to be challenged followed only years later.

And yet I have deliberately left this account of an earlier moment. Of a nanosecond of influence and alignment. Of an error of empathy, if you will. The fact is, I outgrew the empathy. But I remembered for a long time the yearning folded into it. Far from wanting to forget it entirely, I have written this to try to evoke it.

Becoming a poet in the shadow and light of a powerful nationhood is not simple. I imagine a young poet in some other country, standing even now under another window. I imagine them transposing themselves, as I did, into wayward ideas of passion and conviction. It may be they also will come to believe that challenging an inherited tradition—extricating an identity from parts of it—is essential to poetic growth.

And yet my first feelings, as I've described them here, were far more wistful. Withdrawing from those feelings marked the beginning of a series of questions. And yet I could never have framed the questions if I had not known the feelings. I have described the second. I should now try to be precise about the first:

Two words haunted Irish poetry when I was young. Those two pivotal words for an Irish poet—and for many other poets—were *I* and *we*. I have written elsewhere of the broad tensions between these two words, and their meaning for poets in many contexts. But in the Irish context there were specific tensions. These were the words which had been tested by violence and history. These were the poetic pronouns which had followed a century and a country through its ordeals and violations. These were the words which marked new developments in both Irish poem and Irish poet. In the process they, and their relationship to one another, had been profoundly altered.

The word which showed most signs of distress was not the *I*. This was the controversial pronoun, certainly. It was often attacked as denoting autobiography and self-indulgence. It could be a target, even in the self-reflexive Ireland of my time. But there remained something solid about it. It had come through the fire. It sheltered in the poem, a vocal and eloquent witness, well aware of its part in a turbulent Irish history: "I only am escaped alone to tell thee," it seemed to say, like the breathless messenger in the Book of Job.

Not so the *we*. A sub-plot in the poetic history of the late nineteenth and twentieth centuries is surely the story of this pronoun's disintegration. Not just in Ireland, either. In an introduction to an anthology of American Civil War poetry, J. D. McClatchy writes eloquently of the way nineteenth-century poetry still had the power "to turn art's moral light on public matters and private deeds." The words look magical, even now. And yet, with time and uncertainty, whole worlds on which that *we* had once depended—from which it spoke in the poem—had vanished. Entire constituencies were gone. Among them Speranza's Ireland, a nation-state rallied by rhetoric: a community bound to it; and bandaged by it.

But the *I* still existed. It had work to do. It remained at the heart of the enterprise. Only the *we* had faltered. Its hinterland was gone. In Ireland it had enclosed a world of undefeated passion. And now the first-person plural had been swept away with the certainties it sheltered. And because the *I* could no longer depend on that *we*—on its urgent and passionate community—the first-person singular became ever more isolated and contested.

When I stood under the window in Merrion Square I knew nothing of this. Poetry was still an ideal to me: a hoped-for symbiosis of old worlds and new possibilities. The sunderings, the wrenchings of a modern era were not visible. And because I did not know them, for a brief moment I was not bound by them. When I looked up at the lighted rectangle I became a self-styled alchemist on a winter night. In my wistfulness for the old purposes of the public poem, I instinctively acted to hold on to my dream: I re-invented that *I* and joined it to the old *we* of a nationalist Ireland which had long ago ceased to exist. I made a brief, forced re-union of something that had long ago been broken apart.

But there was more to it: there was an inescapable irony. I could stand there, hoping to be an Irish poet, precisely because that *we* had faltered. I, who could never have belonged to Speranza's national aesthetic, was one of the poets who most benefited in my time from the new and private spaces of the modern Irish lyric. In the disintegration of the Irish public poem the future of poets like myself was made possible. And yet I—created by that very opportunity—stood there on a winter night regretting it.

It was an error. And yet I wouldn't be without that error. For that reason, it seems right to record it here: that moment when I first realized a cause and its language could be inseparable. When I tried to go back to a place where poetry followed the drum and had the power to elevate even the casual participant into a hero. If it is a seduction, it is also a source of our self-knowledge—even if it sprang from self-deception. Whether we like it or not, it is part of the history of poetry; part of the biography of the poet. Standing where I did, I stood in the old light of epic and praise-song: places where the art attended to the tribe.

It would take time for me to see the damage these intertwinings can cause. The simplification of Eibhlín Ní Chonaill's legacy is just one example. The way in which a complex achievement was stripped to suit a national purpose is sobering. The way in which a poem was censored in order to make the poet a more reassuring figure is a cautionary tale. In the end, I would find that a national tradition seeks to modify the poet even more than the poem.

And yet ironically it was not the poem I first envied but the poet. It was Speranza. It was that edited version of the public stance which was all the national tradition allowed her; and all she wanted. The role she accepted so readily was made possible by the conjunction between a desperate nationhood and an avid audience.

To my teenage mind, Speranza's identity seemed painlessly constructed. In touch with an audience and in step with history. It was an identity that seemed to reach back to a place where the event and the account of the event were woven from the same cloth. The poet she became knew everything about communality; and nothing at all of the indecision and isolation of a later version of herself. I should know. In many ways, I was that later version. From that perspective, I was right to envy Speranza. And wise to let that envy last for only a short time.

Reading as Intimidation

Our first child was born in winter. The prospect brought us joy and confusion. Our domestic arrangements were casual. Now we needed to re-order them. We planned a simple nursery in an upstairs room. We moved out a guest bed and put in a crib. We painted the walls a flat ivory color. A friend helped us make a dressing table from chipboard with a fabric curtain.

The room was small and cold. It faced north. At dawn the window was slow to let in light. The shelves of the dressing table stood opposite the window and were plainly useful. The fabric of the curtaining was something more. It seemed to promise something far beyond its stopgap role. It showed a woodland with trees and distances. It gazed into the interior as if the soul of some unexpected pastoral had slipped into plainspoken cotton. A few more shelves near the window held books and an ornament or two. Another opposite the door supported an oddly shaped porcelain cat, its skin crazed with blue flowers.

A room like this lasts a short time. My daughter slept away most of her first hard winter. I rose in the dark and warmed a bottle while the garden was gripped by frost. If I thought those magical standstill hours would continue indefinitely, I was wrong. The season relented. Snowdrops appeared under my neighbor's tree. Then yellow crocuses. Then it was spring. The first days of her life were over.

I was prepared for the beauty and intensity of a small child. I became used to the shelter and scale of the room. But I was unprepared for the way it all fused into a drama of arrival and encounter: a continuous daily adventure of sights and insights. I was instructed by them almost without knowing it. I came to see how well the earth and its objects used one another. The light of the morning. The child's first cry. The last star. The hum of the milkman's cart. They played off each other as sounds and sources all day. They stayed in my mind and marked themselves in my memory. And in the midst of all, the new life which made it visible.

But I learned something else as well: a far less radiant subset of knowledge. I found that even in the midst of this adventure and renewal, which had swept away so many human doubts, I was left with my artistic ones. Radical doubts I did not want to have. There in a room at the center of my life they crept in and out—a sort of underhand questioning. The objects on the shelves glowed by lamplight and clarified at dawn. The shape of a milk bottle defined a curve of space. Moonlight stitched itself into the threads of the curtain. Daylight pushed the walls back. And yet the doubts remained.

They were hard to formulate; they were also constant. For all the instruction of that room—its objects and its new life—I was not sure where or whether they belonged in any poem I might write. I had learned this room. But there were other, older learning processes which seemed in conflict with this new knowledge. All that winter these odd thoughts created a fraction of dissonance. A tiny edge of sorrow came to surround them. What use was an expressive medium if it couldn't shelter an expressive life? What purpose was there in giving voice to an old art if it silenced a new experience?

Under those doubts were other ones. A darker version, in fact. I found that without knowing it I had learned to write poetry, at least in part, by subscribing to a hierarchy of poetic subjects. As though I'd signed on to the repertory choices of a summer theater company by conceding to a seasonal imperative. For instance, I understood from the first that a poem had permanent, historic residents. The moon, the horizon, shifts of weather and the color of a field—all signaling an inner life as well as an outer circumstance—belonged in a poem. They could enter it as easily as that pastoral slipped into cotton. As subject matter, their welcome had been arranged by centuries of poetry; by custom, by tradition.

Not so this room. However radiant it seemed to me, it was just a room. There were hundreds, thousands of them marching out into the Irish night, lighting up their yellow windows in the dusk of the Dublin suburbs. The growth of population, the building of estates suggested a social shift; not a poetic change. In this new life I had acquired a subject. But no ready-made importance had been ascribed to it. I had to do that for myself. And yet how could I take this private experience and make it as familiar a poetic subject as a planet or landscape? I could see I would have to do more than write this subject; I would have to authorize it. And here, to my surprise, I faltered.

It was a split-second faltering. A moment of hesitation. Nothing more. But later that moment troubled me. Brief as it was, it remained emblematic. I would think back to it. I would remember it as a painful contradiction—that I doubted the importance of this room as a poetic subject at the very moment I was most convinced of its imaginative power. How could I believe that what was compelling outside the poem might not be equally so inside it?

But I had. And I did. Later, I would wonder how it had happened. I would always come to the same question: What part of the process of becoming a poet had led me to that moment of hesitation? What flaw in my development caused that fissure between feeling and expression?

II

The answer, I knew, had to be more than autobiographical. It needed to be formal as well. I would have to begin there. I was a lyric poet. I thought of myself as one. The description was inexact and I knew there was no precise history for the term. Yet when I thought about it, trusting my identity to that imprecise term, I remembered an incident which made it clearer.

One summer morning, I flew to Manchester to record poems for the BBC. It was a short flight out of Dublin. The program itself was not long. And then I was left with one of those cumbersome units of time: too short to do anything substantive with, too long to spend all of it at the airport waiting for a flight back to Dublin. I went to an art museum. I spent an unsatisfactory hour or so, looking from Pre-Raphaelite paintings to my watch, and back again. Then I went to the museum bookshop, bought one or two catalogues and a pamphlet. And went to the airport early, after all.

Airports are not easy places to inhabit. There is only so much steel, so many rotating wheels and passing luggage carts you can ponder. A coffee; a sandwich wrapped in plastic and seemingly composed of it; another coffee. And then you are ready for something more.

So I reached down and took out the pamphlet from my bag. I hardly knew why I'd chosen it. I must have thought it fitted the bill. Its subject was musical boxes at the Victoria and Albert Museum in London, and it was a bright publication. Glossy, distracting, garrulous. Here were the cylinder musical boxes of the wealthy, fashioned out of pearwood and cast steel with glass lids. Here was a description of a thirteenth-century water clock; a marvel of falcons and chimes and hydraulically operated musicians. And here, wonder of wonders, was the eighteenth-century music box of the Sultan of Mysore.

Then I found something else. In black and white, modestly photographed and with a brief note, was the serinette. Even in monochrome, it was an elaborate affair. A beechwood box, veneered with satinwood, standing on ormolu feet and inlaid with a blonde scroll of songbirds and branches. "Small domestic barrel organs known as serinettes," said the note, "were made in France during the eighteenth century for the express purpose of teaching caged birds to sing."

For a moment I pictured myself in an eighteenth-century drawing room. I imagined the whirl of plaster roses and ceiling cherubs. I could see the fireplace, intricately chiselled out of marble. Everything inlaid, decorated, improved upon. The gatelegs of the dining table would be the only reminder of the broad-leaved trees and the forest which were once the natural element of this caged bird in the corner, who now had to put up with a dome of stale air and brass bars. That and the lid of the satinwood box. Only this, opened now and again—with artificial woodland notes pouring into the room—provided a heartbreaking reminder of freedom.

I will not be oblique about the connection. The small grotesque image of that box lets me argue that the lyric impulse has something in common with the serinette: that it reaches out to a perceptive area which has fallen silent. For the sake of this argument, let me call perception the bird and time the cage. But not just any kind of time or any kind of perception. It must have a real sense of healed possibility, enclosed and entrapped. Time, after all, is a linear configuration. It proceeds from birth to death; or appears to. It encloses us in the inevitability and claustrophobias of mortality. No wonder, then, that a particular perceptive area may fall mute within it. The bird does not sing because it cannot fly.

Was it possible that this is what had happened? That I had entered that small room not just as a new mother, but also as a lyric poet? That the lyric form had signaled to a silence, promising all the time to teach it to speak or sing? And yet had failed to do so. I was reluctant to think so. That same form had brought me into my own life. It had been a steadfast companion. But if its failure was not the cause of my hesitation, what was?

III

Where does it start, the wish to be a poet?

For me it began in teenage years. I went to boarding school in Dublin. The building was perched over the Irish Sea. I could see Howth on a sunny day. At night the moon blinded the dormitory windows with water light.

The surroundings were gracious. But the view of a young woman's future—widespread at that time in Ireland—was not. There was a rigid conservatism about it. Not so much in its emphasis on marriage as in its angers about conformity. There was a fixed circle of suggestions. An unspoken insistence on prescribing limits to the body and mind.

I had no words for it. Definitions were not available. It was an atmosphere, nothing more; and hard to articulate. And yet I'm sure my first reading of poetry took place in its shadow. I may not have been able to name those restrictions. But I felt them: I even recognized them as a kind of repression. I also realized, in some unspeaking way, that I could not yet rescue my body. I was years away from that. But I could rescue my mind. I set out to do so.

And so I established a pattern of what I will call here reading as intimidation. I read poems then as I never did again: as a method of self-protection. I read them to persuade myself of something the climate seemed about to deny me. There was nothing wrong with the poems. Some of them, I could see, had reach, beauty, relevance. But I chose them for the wrong reasons. With the result they had the wrong effect: I had no idea that by taking poems out of context, using them as armor against invidious assumptions, I might intimidate myself out of a sense of my own reality.

I see myself again at fourteen years of age. I am staring at the pages of an anthology. The book is worn. The pages are thin and missal-fine. They slip and rustle as I turn them. There is even an old-fashioned silky ribbon to mark the pages. The sleeves of my school cardigan are pushed up. My index finger has inkwell stains on it. Out beyond the window the Irish Sea is turning to a metallic color at dusk. The landmass is disappearing. The visible signs of a country are turning to shadows. It doesn't matter. They hardly existed for me even when visible. It will be years before I allow those shapes beyond the page to enter and inform the poem on it.

And here I am struggling with a single poem. The poet is English. He is long dead, much admired—an icon of the English canon. All prescriptions for a profound disconnect. I am Irish, at the painful end of puberty, unable to read my own body or know my own nation. And here is John Dryden, able to decipher everything, or so it seems. The poem is "A Song for St. Cecilia's Day."

> FROM harmony, from heavenly harmony,
>   This universal frame began:
> When nature underneath a heap
>   Of jarring atoms lay,
> And could not heave her head,
> The tuneful voice was heard from high,
>   "Arise, ye more than dead!"
> Then cold, and hot, and moist, and dry,
> In order to their stations leap,
>   And Music's power obey.

As I read, I fail to understand why a man whose life is touched by a civil war would write this slide of rhymes and sounds. Nevertheless, I apply myself to the poem, to its abstract and seemingly cold celebration of music. To its cosmology, which I can't understand, and its religion, which was, at the very moment of its composition, wreaking havoc on my own country.

Ironically, this will all change. Later in life I will come to admire the poem deeply. I will relish Dryden's use of Pythagorean theory to dazzle Platonic thought. Written by this eldest of fourteen children, at fifty-six years of age, who has seen his country broken by war, what I once mistook for coldness I will come to see as a heart-wrenching yearning for order. But I don't see that. I am fourteen years of age, determined to master what small worlds of meaning I can. And so I am reading the poem to gain its power and protection. By doing so, I am missing its point.

And so here it is. An act of reading that becomes a method of intimidation. An act self-selected because I am already intimidated. These are not easy matters to explain. They are fragmentary, lost in a mercurial past and a still more mercurial thought process.

Nevertheless, I can find my way back to some of it, even now. The fact is, I am turning in circles in those years. I am trying to break free by disputing a prediction. In my reading, I go instinctively to big subjects that take me away from small concerns. In a culture which warns that the treasures and complications of the mind might be beyond the reach of a young woman, I instinctively look for texts that seem to promise their availability. And I select difficult poems because I feel clever and safe reading them.

This is not, I know, an orthodox account of a poet's early reading. It is more usual to provide a narrative of grace: of encountering language and form for the first time. Which did happen; but later. Nevertheless, this earlier, darker version, I am convinced, is less uncommon than it looks. "Reading is a very complex art," wrote Virginia Woolf. Of one thing I am sure: There must have been other young women who read for their own protection. Who were agents of their own intimidation. Who chose poems, as I did, not because they brought them nearer to the life of feeling but because they removed them safely from it. Who felt that the power and distance of language would protect them from the limitations made ready for them.

None of it lasted. Soon enough I set aside this way of reading and took up the poems of Yeats. But I have remembered my first choices here; and my reasons for them. Later I would trace these strange, small aberrations stubbornly to their source. I would try to align them with ideas and forms. I would go back to the same question: Where did the lyric form come in? Had it helped or hindered? After all, as I remembered it, I had stood in that room alone with my child, at a moment of intense personal history. Surely the history of the lyric should have coincided with it.

IV

And the lyric has a considerable history. It has proved itself to be endlessly adaptable to new environments and changing circumstances. It seems fair to ask, Why didn't it adapt to mine, at once and unquestioningly?

The answer is complex; the question itself may be off-kilter. We are looking at a form which has fitted itself, on different occasions, to the lyre, to the lute, to the harp. To the small kingdom and the lost tribe. Anyone could find it, if they searched, on the Pyramid texts in Egypt. Under the battlements in Picardy. On the back roads of Ireland in a defeated language. It doesn't always occur in the same shape, and rarely in the same words. But it is recognizably the same creature we glimpse. As if we could deduce a mythical animal by its foot-print in the snow of high places.

The Irish, like other European nations, have marched and wept and kept their faith and their counsel to the sound and stress of lyrics. William Yeats even floated the idea that the Irish sensibility was better suited to the lyric than the English one. In "A General Introduction for My Work" he wrote about his own early decision to write short poems: he spoke of the Irish preference for "a swift current."

That's not to say the lyric hasn't had its detractors. "Nothing is capable of being well set to music that is not nonsense," wrote the critic Joseph Addison. And today, when the lyric is no longer set to music, his skepticism is still around. Critics have needed little encouragement—especially if, like Addison, they suffer from a surfeit of reason—to take a reductive view of it. To regard it as a pretty and prettified segment of poetic expression. A fossil of times and occasions when the poem was the expressive equivalent of the sweetmeat.

And yet, as a form, its roots go far deeper than fashion or folly. The *Princeton Encyclopedia of Poetry and Poetics* awarded it the most compelling history of all: "At that remote point in time when syllables ceased to be nonsense and became syntactically and connotatively meaningful the first lyric was composed."

There could hardly be a more profound destiny for a form than this: to be a document of the line between language and its negation; to be a venerable witness. It gives the lyric the dignity of having been one of the first theaters of meaning. When a formation is so powerful, so deep in time and history, it is not likely to be erased later. The first lyrics articulated, among other things, the human need for self-expression under the stress of a struggle for existence. We have no exact record of that need. Whatever record there might be is inscribed, not in a book or a chronicle, but in that part of our psyches which corresponds to the listening memory of the caged linnet.

And so, in the end, I stopped suspecting the lyric. It had not failed me. It was not the form which was responsible for my silence. In fact the opposite. In hunting down reasons for that moment of hesitation, I came to believe something quite different. Gradually, I became sure that a rogue history of ideas—the very same which shaped my early reading—had stood between me and the poem I wanted to write. But what was it?

V

Every poet has an anti-history. A place where some turn was taken that seemed to put the future in doubt. I had my anti-history. I found it early and kept it late. For me it was that insistence on elevated subject matter described, among others, by Edmund Burke: "Vast Objects occasion vast Sensations," he wrote, "and vast Sensations give the Mind a higher Idea of her own Powers." It was, in other words, the arc of the sublime—its argument and emphasis—woven in and through all kinds of poems and histories of poems. I resisted it; and I had reasons for doing so.

To start with, I was Irish. I was a woman. Once I left school and began to write, I was a poet whose life was lived among the objects of an ordinary existence. It was a safer life than most; and similar to many of the lives lived around me. I wrote my poems upstairs in a room that looked out to a garden. My notebook stayed on a table during the day while I saw to small children. At night with the closing in of the dark, I could go back to writing.

But when I took up a pen, or faced the blank page of my notebook, I understood certain things: I was free to live my life. Compared with many other women, in far more limiting circumstances, I was fortunate. And yet one question kept coming back: I was free to live my life. But was I free to imagine it? Did the poems I had read, or the poetic tradition I had inherited, encourage me to do that? Did the history of these ideas of the sublime suggest I could live in an eye-level relation to the objects I saw every day around me? Or did something whisper when I took up my pen—*What are you writing? Is it important enough?* I felt a need to critique my doubts. The critique of my doubts inevitably ended in criticism of the sublime. But what did that mean?

It certainly did not mean poring over Longinus or Edmund Burke. If anything, I read them in a glancing way. Some sentences and fragments escaped me; some stayed with me. "For, as if instinctively, our soul is uplifted by the true sublime; it takes a proud flight" wrote Longinus. And yet it was not those words which defined the hollowness of the sublime for me. Nor John Dennis, nor the Earl of Shaftesbury, nor Addison.

If it was not those writers and writing I resisted, what was it? The answer was imprecise at one level, but painfully clear to me on another. It was an ethos more than an argument. A slow bending of space. A curving of the scale and size of the poet. It was a painting here, an essay there, a collection of symbols and a growing assent to them. It was a series of brushstrokes, putting the human traveler as small as could be on the ridge of the hill and making the waterfall into an image as big as a dinosaur. It was a series of propositions that seemed to gather force, like an opposing headwind, throughout the nineteenth century. It was not just Kant's "supersensible state" and Hegel's "sublated" means. It was a magic show willingly put on by painters, poets, musicians which made man small and the world large.

The magic show was deceptive; the magicians were hidden. When you looked more closely, a sort of sleight of hand was happening. In reality, the sublime was not an idea that cut the poet down to size. In fact the opposite. It was an idea *made* by the poet. And so, throughout the show, the poet was behind the curtain, defining the very grandeur he appeared to be awed by, and in the process becoming a steward of it. And so a new kind of poet emerged: A master of secrets, a controller of meaning. And, of course, a stakeholder in perpetuating that grandeur.

VI

And so I arrived at my answer. It was not the lyric form that failed me. It was something else: a current of ideas and insistences on which the lyric poem was buoyant, in which it had never capsized. And yet that stream of ideas—I have called it the sublime here—had been powerful enough to intimidate me as a teenager. It stood beside me as a ghost of meaning, warning and promising about the significance of inherited knowledge and the fearful diminishment of my own reading and writing if I did not seek its sanction. And it was powerful enough to make me hesitate for that fraction of time when I entered the room in which my first child slept.

The attempt to track back from that small hesitation brought me some questions and a few answers. I have tried to include them here. Writing about these remembered states is elusive. They are so quickly over, so poorly defined that they become like an old photograph. We look at it closely. We're nearly sure that was the tree we saw from the window. We almost believe that was the neighbor who came in to borrow the shears. But the moment is gone.

And yet it all connects up. Recalling my forced connection with poetry at the age of fourteen made me remember a skepticism about the sublime which came later. Locating myself, even at a young age, in a place where great knowledge made a personal world seem small might look like a common human circumstance. And a world away from the glorious antechamber of the sublime—so argued about, so adhered to from Burke to Poe. But there was a link. I was sure of it.

Coming forward from that time to the most personal moment of a personal world—the existence of a new child— I see again a slim and unproveable connection. Nothing was more important to me than this new life. Yet it had a human scale. It was a small event, however momentous to me. I knew those events registered in the ideology of the sublime as simply ones to be warned against. Unfortunately the girl I was, reading Dryden in a school library, was willing to be warned. The woman I became, entering my child's room, might hesitate for a moment, remembering that warning. But not for long.

When I was young I thought of aesthetics as an abstract code. I learned later it was a human one. I learned it belongs everywhere, and to no one person. Which means it can be a common possession. Standing in a room in the winter half-light before the wonder of a new child is aesthetics. Hesitating at the meaning of subject matter as fit for poetry is aesthetics. Searching back to the prompts and resistances involved in becoming a poet—the reading, the writing—is also aesthetics. I came to believe there is no meaning to an art form with its grand designs unless it allows the humane to shape the invented, the way gravity is said to bend starlight.

Translating the Underworld

A few years ago, I came on an anthology of German poetry. I had begun working on a translation project. It involved German-speaking women poets before and during the Second World War. It was not a dutiful undertaking. I had my own reasons for doing it. They came from childhood.

After the war, when I was a small child and lived in Dublin, two German girls—they were sisters—came to live in our house. The cities they left behind were still struggling in the aftermath of war. There was some sanctuary for them in leaving. Ireland had rationing but there was meat and butter available. Compared with other countries, food was fresh and plentiful.

The sisters were young, still teenagers. They helped my mother with the children. They tried to teach us German—

phrases, numbers. *Ich bin beschäftigt. Eine zwei drei vier fünf.*
Mostly they learned English and used it every day in faltering,
heavily accented voices. I was too young at first to hear or
understand them. Later I understood more. When my parents left the room they talked to each other in rapid, headlong
German. As I remember it, as I hear it again now, it was a dialect of pure homesickness. Even now I can see and hear our
kitchen in Dublin: twilight at the windows, steam rising from
damp clothes and, in the midst of it all, their voices.

Later, I would think of those lapses into pain and language
as more than just signals between sisters. Later it seemed that
the door they opened was legendary, not real—that it led from
our teatime kitchen into the very heart of a broken Europe.
And the conduit, the path was language. A language I could
not understand but which spoke to me all the same. And there
it stayed, a fraction of mystery and displacement. An intaglio:
something cut into my mind but neither available or clear.

It was there when I returned from the university book-
store one evening in California, carrying an anthology of
German poetry. I opened the pages to the contemporary section. Despite my childhood—and the fact that I heard German spoken for years in our house—my knowledge of the
language was now almost nonexistent. Whatever there had
been was now mostly forgotten.

And yet as I began looking at the anthology I found that not
quite everything was gone. There was a sort of half-light of
sounds and words through which I could peer: a dusk of linguistic memories. What made it possible for me to look at the
page was that, if I listened in some inward way, I could hear an
echo-language as I first heard it. Then the sounds of the two
sisters would come back—whole phrases, a harsh music. The
idiom and syntax were beyond me. Nevertheless, there was

something—a shadow of auditory comprehension—which allowed me to keep reading.

The book I was reading was one of several. They were scattered on the table. I was at the stage of making notes. This particular anthology, as it happened, had hardly any contemporary poets. I turned idly to the last few poets in the book. One of the most recent—a woman—was born in 1899. She was represented by a single poem. I was about to close the book when something caught my eye. The poet, Elisabeth Langgässer, had chosen a date as the title of her poem. *Frühling 1946*. Spring 1946. The year those sisters came to us. The small coincidence struck home. Just enough to stop me from putting the book aside. I began to read.

It was a short, dense poem. Six stanzas. Five lines to each stanza. Its subject was the return of spring. The first line was an invocation to the anemone flower. *Holde Anemone. Sweet Anemone.* Spring was returning, the lines said, the flower was opening. As I read it, checking against the English prose transliteration at the bottom of the page, I remembered something. This must be the white meadow-anemone I had heard of once—the flower of dry uplands. It was more than a wildflower. It was a simple, a healing plant. I read and re-read the first stanza.

> *Holde Anemone,*
> *Bist du wieder da*
> *Und erscheinst mit heller Krone*
> *Mir Geschundenem zum Lohne*
> *Wie Nausikaa?*

The anthology made no attempt at a poetic translation. I had to refer to the brief, arcane prose crib at the bottom of the page. It was helpful, of course. It was also clumsy and somehow demeaning with its eccentric syntax. (*So you are back again, gracious anemone, and coming up with bright calyx, to comfort me for my bruises like Nausicaa.*)

From the start I was puzzled . Enough to keep taking the book up and putting it down. Enough to go on worrying it for the rest of the evening. That first stanza, for instance: There was something odd about it. It invoked a flower. But then it seemed to change course. Like a Hollywood action hero leaping from building to building, it jumped from flower to myth: from the anemone to Nausicaa. On the page, it looked like a conventional lyric poem. So why do that?

That wasn't all. "Most of us don't live lives that lend themselves to novelistic expression, because our lives are so fragmented," stated Tobias Wolff in an interview. His comment is apt here. The fragments were extreme. The poem was trying to catch them. And yet even its background seemed like a doctored photograph: *Springtime 1946*. The title was explicit. It evoked images of the harsh, lunar landscape of Berlin in the immediate aftermath of war. Women standing with handcarts and headbands. Carrying away rubble. Broken windows opening back into freezing apartments. Hunger and humiliation: the bitter aftermath of defeat. Surely a bizarre series of associations for a poem whose self-styled identity seemed to be that of a graceful German pastoral poem.

A few nights later, I went to the library. I found the German section. In the gloom behind the main stacks, there was a handful of books by or about Elisabeth Langgässer. And there, just like that, my search—still at a take-it-or-leave-it stage—struck home.

On the floor-level shelves I came on two stoutly bound

books. They were called *Briefe*. I looked at the library stamps on the back inside cover. Hardly anyone had ever taken them out. Langgässer's letters. I pulled down a dictionary. I took them to a corner of the library and started to look through them.

I knew nothing about this woman. I hardly knew why I was there. And yet even with my dictionary and a painful lack of idiomatic German, I had to admit that by now I was drawn in. Even the layout of the pages revealed something. I needed no idiom, for instance, to see that Langgässer was a generous, invincible letter writer. There were pages and pages of greetings. *Meine Liebe Camilla. Liebe Waldemar. Sehr geehrter Herr Winterhalter!* The letters covered a quarter of a century. This was a woman who relished friendship and made the best of distance.

But I was not looking for the friend or neighbor who wrote some of these letters. I was looking for the poet. I turned to the year 1946. Since the poem was titled for the spring of that year, maybe the letters would point to the reason for it. Here, surely, there would be a clue. I turned to the first letter of 1946. It was written on the Feast of the Epiphany, and so marked: January 6, 1946.

And there it was. Just one sentence at the top of the letter. *Cordelia lebt! Cordelia is alive.* I had found it. The letter went into further detail and I would study that and try to untangle the implications. But for now I had a name and a revelation. Cordelia. Not Anemone. Not Nausicaa. Not the codes of a lyric poem. But a real name. I had found the one sentence that could be joined with the poem. It was a simple enough deduction, made out of curiosity and logic. The poem was dated. The letters were dated too. But it was not curiosity and logic that I felt, sitting in the dusk of the library. It was something deeper and less rational. Here for me, with that one sentence, a project turned into a passion.

II

Elisabeth Langgässer was born in 1899 in the busy market town of Alzey, not far from Mainz, near the wine-producing area of Rheinhessen in southwestern Germany. The houses were half-timbered. The public buildings had rosy, picturesque roofs. Even today, in photographs, there are remnants of the old fish markets.

She was baptized Catholic. Her mother was Christian. She herself was raised as a Catholic. Her architect father, Eduard Langgässer, was Jewish. His racial and religious identity would have profound consequences for her.

There are photographs of Langgässer as a child. She is dark-eyed and strong-jawed in them. She stands by the knee of elderly parents. Huge potted plants, long skirts and her father's sideburns mark out an old-fashioned European moment. Here in the town of the *Fastnacht*—the Shrove Tuesday procession—where small fillets and fish were served and custom was preserved, it would be quiet for a while before the storm.

In the first photos, she is a young girl. Then a teenager, wearing glinting spectacles. Then a young woman. Now something else emerges. An air of elegance. A studious and yet elusive sexual confidence. During these years she qualified as a teacher and between 1921 and 1924 she taught elementary school in Griesheim and Darmstadt. She was already writing.

Her first volume of poems, *Der Wendekreis des Lammes*, was published in 1924.

It was in Griesheim in 1928 that she met Hermann Heller, who had fought on the Eastern Front and was then forty years of age. He was also Jewish. Their brief relationship resulted in Langgässer becoming pregnant. In 1929 a daughter, Cordelia, was born. The child took her father's name, and was registered as Cordelia Heller. In the same year, Langgässer moved to Berlin with her mother and grandmother.

It was the second and third stanzas of "Frühling 1946" which captured me. I began to translate them tentatively. The cadences were rhythmical—in English they would be trimester and tetrameter, angled together so as to make a lyric march; at times, a strung-out symphony of triumphant line endings and easements. In the third stanza it becomes a force-field of sounds:

> *Sah in Gorgos Auge*
> *Eisenharten Glanz,*
> *Ausgesprühte Lügenlauge*
> *Hört' ich flüstern, daß sie tauge*
> *Mich zu töten ganz.*

The prose translation, as elsewhere, was cryptic and awkward: *I saw the steely hard gleam in the Gorgon's eye I heard lies' squirted venom whisper that she could tell me utterly.*

I made a translator's decision. I would not follow this rhythm precisely. A gifted young scholar, Alys George, who was fluent in German had helped me with other translations from the German. One afternoon she recited "Frühling 1946" for me in German. As I heard it out loud, the poem was nuanced and charged. But how to carry that over? The particular torsion of tetameter and trimeter in English is not anguished in that way. On the contrary, it bustles along with the cadence of a Victorian song; the sort of sound-verse that might be found in a British imperial encyclopedia—hubris-stirring and hopelessly out of sync with the poem. My first attempts faltered for that reason. I realized they wouldn't work. And so I went back and shadowed the rhythm as best I could, but in a more open and voice-driven way:

> *I have seen the iron gleam*
> *in the Gorgon's eye.*
> *I have heard the hiss, the whisper,*
> *the rumor that she would kill me:*
> *It was a lie.*

And then, once again, I came to a dead end. What Gorgon? What eye so hard and what whisper so venomous? I looked back at the strange and brief biographical note in the anthology where I found the poem. *Elisabeth Langgässer, 1899–1950: A Rhineland Catholic. Besides novels and short stories she wrote nature poetry in the style of Loerke and Lehmann, using fresh and startling mythological imagery.* I looked through the other notes. They were brief also. But not one of them, right back to the fifteenth century, referred to the writer's religion. A small glitter of meaning passed in front of me; and disappeared again.

III

And now I want to disrupt this story. To stand back from it. To question the very process I was so intent on—the translation of a poem. The truth was I had never seen myself as a natural translator. A grateful reader; but not a practitioner.

And yet like many poets who began writing in the sixties, I owed a great debt to poetry in translation. Without it, I would never have found Montale or Mayakovsky. Or, for that matter, Akhmatova and Fortini. Those poets, carried over into English, meant a widening of my horizons. I lived in Dublin. I was an Irish poet. The intensity of the Irish literary tradition was both nourishing and suffocating.

But at the end of the day I could escape. I could turn away from the choking richness of my own atmosphere and take down the small paperbacks published by Chatto and Jonathan Cape—available only here and there in Dublin bookshops— and begin to read.

Then there would come to me, in a Dublin twilight, a Russian woman standing outside a prison. Waiting patiently in the iron cold of that winter. Or I could enter the lushness and danger of a Hitlerian spring and read Montale. Or right there, in my front room, in a house at the foothills of temperate mountains, Pasternak's snow blizzard would show itself, "sculptured on the glass."

And so I depended in those years on the enterprise of translation: on the selection process that brings words and cadences from one language to another. In some sense, I took it for granted. It was, I felt, a necessary gift; even an inevitable one. Never once, reading Akhmatova's Epilogue to *Requiem* or Fortini's "Lightnings of the Magnolia" did it occur to me that there was a shadow side. I assumed that rites of passage were also routes of travel: that what was worthwhile would come through.

I look back now and it makes an odd image. Here I am, newly married, in a suburban house at the edge of Dublin.

I wear the clothes of that moment; I live comfortably in my own time, in my own skin. The dusks outside the window are full of grit and salt. The autumn air smells of peat and coal. Upstairs my own notebook waits—a blue school copybook, propped open with a cheap pen beside it.

And there, just outside the line of sight, is a small book. It hardly matters whether it's Tsvetayeva or Rilke. What matters is the yearning and lack of understanding with which I pick it up. Snow dusts the pages of Pasternak. A hard, arid light comes from Cavafy. Montale's work looks to the Mediterranan. And still the Irish dusk insists on its enclosures and limits.

So far so good. But I will continue the disruption, in order to show the shadow side of the enterprise of translation. For all the pieties that attend it, for all the knowledge that we depend on it as poets and readers, there is a presumption involved in taking a poem from one language to another, from one vision to another. And certainly, I felt deeply uncomfortable in the very act of translating "Frühling 1946." Even as I puzzled over the stanzas, the idioms, I felt a self-accusing self-awareness: a subtle shifting of translator into intruder which seemed beyond my control. What was I doing here? I asked myself. I was Irish. I was not German. I was not Jewish. I could represent the words of a woman who had lost her daughter. But could I ever imagine her suffering? Of course not—at least not within that cauldron of history. Someone else should do this, I said to myself. I said it over and over. But one fact kept staring back at me. No one else had.

I believe now those were the wrong questions. Translators are not the keepers of history or the interpreters of circumstance. They have a more modest charge: they are simply escorts. Bringing meaning from one language to the other.

And maybe not even that. When I was doubtful, I remembered the defiant words of the Irish poet Biddy Jenkinson:
"I would prefer not to be translated into English in Ireland,"
she stated. "It is a small rude gesture to those who think that
everything can be harvested and stored without loss in an
English-speaking Ireland."

At the end of the day, I recognized that my unease did not
matter. What mattered was that the poem needed a translator.
There may have been other translations in English; but I could
not find them. And I wanted this poem to be found. It was
beautiful, compelling and seemed somehow larger than itself.
And so I applied the one credential I possessed—superseding
history, language, war or retrospect: This was a lyric poem. I
was a lyric poet. And so I continued.

IV

It was the fifth stanza of the poem which had sent me to the
letters.

> *Anemone! Küssen*
> *Laß mich dein Gesicht:*
> *Ungenspiegelt von den Flüssen*
> *Styx und Lethe, ohne Wissen*
> *um das Nein und Nicht.*

This is the place where the poem swerves to its true subject. The tenderness of tone—so powerful, so tense—now
becomes clear. *Let me kiss your face.* All at once, the flower has
become a child. The cadences are intact. The enjambment
softens into statement:

Anemone, my daughter,
let me kiss your face: it is
unmirrored by the waters
of Lethe or of Styx.
And innocent of no or not.

Langgässer was a traditional poet—a lyric discipline marks
"Frühling 1946." The other German women poets of her time
or earlier—Elsa Lasker-Schüler, for instance—follow a different path. Both Nelly Sachs and Lasker-Schüler were aware of
the fractured world recorded by poets like Paul Celan. They
mirrored it in certain of their poems. There is a heartbro-
ken speech they refuse to organize into musical symmetry.
But that is not Langgässer. She is not experimental, at least
not in this poem. "Frühling 1946" is shrewdly, carefully built;
stanza to stanza. I was drawn in by the lyric caution, the jeweled structure. But I remained troubled. There remained one
inconsistency to the discipline, the caution. Most lyric poems
proceed along the lines of imagistic logic. Then why would
an orderly lyric poet make that odd disconcerting leap—from
Anemone to Nausicaa?

There had to be a reason for this shift. Yet the distance
from a small meadow flower to a character in Homer's *Odyssey* seemed more like a detour than a journey. A disconnect
in fact. And yet I had developed an odd faith in the poem. I
decided to try again—this time just following the reference.

Nausicaa: Maybe if I took her out of the flat dimensions
of a myth, I thought, she would offer a clue. She enters
Homer's *Odyssey* at a crucial moment. She is a Phaeacian
princess. She goes to the beach to wash her clothes. Odysseus
stumbles onto her island, having been shipwrecked by the
god Poseidon—"brine gushing from his mouth and nostrils."

Nausicaa and her women are at the edge of the shore and they find him. Nausicaa gives him food and drink, and brings him to the palace of her father.

I went over the story carefully. I mapped it onto my mind. Then onto my sense of the poem: Nausicaa saves Odysseus. She is the bridge across which Odysseus can resume the journey home. The shipwreck has been arranged by the gods. And they arrange the outcome—a series of surprises and blessings. So when Nausicaa and Odysseus make their farewells to each other, they are mutually eloquent about the coincidence and rescue. "I will never fail to worship you all the rest of my days. For it was you who gave me back my life," says Odysseus. Then Nausicaa says, "Good luck, my friend . . . and I hope that when you are in your own country you will remember me at times, since it is to me before all others that you owe your life."

I stared at Homer's lines. *I hope that when you are in your own country you will remember me.* I went back to the poem. The connection between the speaker and Nausicaa is not really disclosed in Langgässer's poem. But the hints of rescue are seamed into the poem's beginning and end. When the poem opens, the last line of the first stanza gathers all the references of healing and puts it into a two-word last line (*wie Nausikaa*)— like Nausicaa. The first lines of the next stanza, with their references to wind and spray and light (*Woge, Schaum und Licht!*), continue the reference.

I was intrigued. But not much closer. The lovely, cryptic poem seemed shut into secrets as well as mysteries. The theme of returning spring was clear. The idea of a child returning was also clear. But a girl at the edge of a mythic ocean, saving a life, directing someone homewards—what was that?

I was about to find out.

V

I was frustrated at the lack of information. Seven years ago Internet searches were more cumbersome and less complete. If there was a large body of commentary on Langgässer I couldn't access it. The Swedish film director Stefan Jarl's admirable film project *Das Mädchen aus Auschwitz* (*The Girl from Auschwitz*) was not yet in existence. I could find little enough.

And then I found another clue. By following on fragments and hints, I stumbled on a harrowing memoir. The reference to it turned up after searching other books. I sent away for the memoir and began reading it the same day it arrived. Immediately it seemed to me an extraordinary testament.

The memoir is called *Burned Child Seeks the Fire*. This is its English title. It was first published in 1984 in Sweden under the title *Bränt barn söker sig till elden*. It came out in Germany as *Gebranntes Kind sucht das Feuer* in 1987. Finally in 1998 it was published by Beacon Press in the United States in an eloquent translation by Joel Agee.

The book is searing and luminous. In short episodes and nonlinear evocations, it calls up a Berlin childhood, the lengthening shadow of Nazi domination and the figure of Elisabeth Langgässer. And this is where the story turns. The author is Cordelia Edvardson, Langgässer's daughter. She is the child to whom "Frühling 1946" is addressed. She is Anemone. She is Nausicaa.

Cordelia Heller was Langgässer's first child. When her brief affair with a married Jewish teacher in 1929 resulted in a pregnancy, Langgässer, against custom, kept her infant daughter. With her mother and her brother she moved to Berlin, away from the small town where a single mother might be less acceptable.

The child's first memories are of a dark apartment in Berlin-Siemensstadt. Her mother is the dominant presence: "Not for anything in the world would she have wanted to miss even a single one of the shining moments when her mother revealed herself and entered into her life." But then in 1933 the family's circumstances changed again. Langgässer met and married Wilhelm Hoffmann. Their marriage was problematic, since in 1935 the Nuremberg Laws were passed against the Jews, prohibiting, among other things, any inter-religious marriage. Although Langgässer was a Catholic in name, she was considered Jewish under the new laws. Hoffmann was not Jewish. "Perhaps it was not even by chance," the memoir states, "that outwardly he corresponded to the archetype of 'The Aryan,' the pure unsullied hero of Wagner's opera."

In the same year, Langgässer was prohibited from writing by the Nazi Reich Literature Chamber. She was expelled from the *Reichsschrifttumskammer*, the equivalent of the Writers Union. This amounted to a professional disqualification, cutting her off from income as well as publication. Between 1933 and 1941 Langgässer had more children, three small daughters.

By 1940, the Nazis had extended their reach. Cordelia Heller, as a *Volljüdin*, was required to wear the yellow star and live away from home. Langgässer was spared. As the deportations intensified, Langgässer managed to get a Spanish passport for her daughter. It was an ingenious and dangerous maneuver. And it failed. Langgässer and Cordelia were summoned to Gestapo headquarters in Berlin. What happened then is at the heart of the memoir: it registers the scalding separation of mother and child. It also records the emergence of Nausicaa: the piece has a terrible eloquence. It is almost unbearable reading.

But, and the word sounded like the crack of a whip, but if you do not sign on the spot, we will have to prosecute your mother! He told the girl that the mother had arranged the daughter's Spanish adoption in order to circumvent German laws, which could be regarded as a serious offense, as treason, high treason, and some third category which the girl was later unable to remember. However, if the girl signed now, no harm would be done, and the mother's lapse could he excused. And he added, just to be sure: You are no doubt aware of the fact that your mother is a half-Jew. Again the daughter looked at the mother and met with the gaze of her beautiful brown eyes, eyes that shone with intensity, that knew how to cast a spell on the girl, but which now were full to the brim with wordless, helpless pain. No one said anything, nothing needed to be said, there was no choice, there never had been, she was Cordelia, who kept her vow of fidelity, she was also Proserpine, she was the chosen one, and never had she felt closer to her mother's heart. Her voice was choked, but finally she got the words out: Yes, I'll sign?

VI

Some years ago, I was part of a poetry seminar in Kraków. One afternoon I made the short journey to Auschwitz. The space between Auschwitz and Auschwitz-Birkenau travels across open country. It has high skies. Someone on the bus told me it was perfect country for larks. To these rooms, to these angles and distances, and to this out-of-reach lark song, Cordelia Heller was brought in the winter of 1942.

It was hard to credit in this barren, quiet landscape how much human evil had taken shape there. It was hard to comprehend the rooms, the photographs, the evidence of suffering and murder. And yet Cordelia Heller entered it at its worst moment. At the age of fifteen, she was forced to become an assistant to Josef Mengele, the so-called angel of death. She stood on the platform beside him. She made and kept lists in the *Selektionem* process. She took down the names of those whom Mengele decided should survive, signaling his decision with a thumb up or down behind his back.

By the time I came to Auschwitz-Birkenau I was a captive of both poem and memoir. Both seemed to me beautiful, essential texts. They also seemed less heralded than they should be. I thought of each of them in different ways. But chiefly I thought of the teenager who stepped, as a poet's child—as the future subject of "Frühling 1946"—into this terrain of evil. She describes it in this way:

> Mengele and Mandel. Mandel and Mengele. The blonde camp commandant Maria Mandel in Auschwitz-Birkenau and the dark-haired Dr. Mengele, who carried out the selections. The King and Queen of the Realm of the Dead where the girl had been brought.

Despite the terrible sadness of the place, I wanted more detail. Our guide was Polish. I asked her about the selection process and told her I had read a memoir whose author had been part of it. I said this author mentioned keeping lists and noting down names. She explained there could be no traces of this in Auschwitz-Birkenau. The evidence had been destroyed as the Soviet army approached. But in Auschwitz itself, some evidence remained: the notes existed of an earlier selection process. Under a glass case, I saw neatly written names, carefully inscribed in small handwriting on paper.

> The fate of the other women was literally decided behind their backs. Mengele . . . would scrutinize them for a moment, they would turn right and march off, towards another SS man who was standing a few meters away, and behind their backs the sign would be given: thumb up or thumb down.

Only rarely in the book is the full relation between daughter and mother discussed, and then mostly in mythical terms.

> But there was something she would take with her on her way, Ariadne's thread which her mother had given her, the thread of the fairy tale, of the myth, and the poem, fine as silk and, it was said, stronger than death. But the girl also knew that this thread she had received from her mother, the unsevered umbilical cord, would lead her where she did not want to go, to the gate of the realm of the dead.

VII

This is not a piece about history. Nor even an argument about the past. If anything, it is intended as a commentary on translation; a scribble in the margin of the great enterprise of bringing poetry from one language to another. It is about that moment when a poet who has seen the world in one language finds it again in another. It is a perilous and crucial process. As I worked with "Frühling 1946," I looked for and was often struck by poets' comments on their own translating experience. They gave guidance and a sort of comfort.

In one of his Clark lectures, for instance, Charles Tomlinson spoke of "transfusing" the "soul of your original." Willis Barnstone wrote that "a translation is a friendship between poets." The Irish-language poet Seán Ó'Riordáin hinted at a motive for the process when he said, "A person must keep traveling from self to self."

And yet what do we want from a poem in translation? What do we see when we look at a poem whose origin is in a language—and therefore a history and an ethos—which is not ours. A window? A mirror? And what does the poem deserve from us? Certainly there is a need for empathy as well as accuracy. In a poignant comment, Carolyn Forché said in an interview, "You almost become that poet while you are translating."

But there is also the integrity of the work to be considered—the pure intent. I recalled Edward Hirsch's eloquent comment in *Blood to Remember*, an anthology of Holocaust elegies: "I just wanted to write a poem that would speak about the experience from inside—from inside and outside of language, from inside and outside of history, from inside and outside of human life." It is what any translator would want to do.

"Frühling 1946" forced me to think about something else: the relation of a poem to the narrative it espouses. There is an angle of disconnection between Langgässer's poem and her daughter's memoir. Cordelia Edvardson mentions many aspects of Langgässer in *Burned Child Seeks the Fire*. She never mentions the poem. But what consideration does a translator owe to missing references and inferences?

In the end I surprised myself by the depth of loyalty I felt to both poem and memoir. Its best expression, it seemed to me, was not to confuse them. *Burned Child Seeks the Fire*— although it is often poetic—is a narrative. "Frühling 1946" is a lyric. As a reader I might have questions about the reach of the poem. As a translator I could not. The self-imposed limits of the poem are the self-prescribed obligations of the translator.

A woman stands over an abyss. She finds her child has survived the worst of history. She takes up pen and paper and records the moment. But the moment refuses to be contained. It flows out and beyond the poem into story and consequence. Looked at from that story and those consequences, the poem appears incomplete. But was it? Is it?

I don't believe so. The poem is a note from the underworld. It is the first signal from Ceres that she has found her child. All the rest can come later.

VIII

There is a fragment of narrative left. Cordelia was rescued by the Swedish Red Cross. It took time to sort out names, addresses, and to locate her in hospital. Finally, on the Feast of the Epiphany her mother sat down to write the words I first read in the library. *Cordelia lebt!*

But the darkness was far from over. By the time she wrote the letter, Elisabeth Langgässer was ill with multiple sclerosis. She died in 1950. She and her daughter met only briefly in the remaining time. And the poem and the memoir do not meet at all.

But that is not what this is about. This is about a single, small act of translation—and my hopes and concerns while I was involved in it. Nevertheless, the story itself left an indelible mark. So often the references to myth can be decorative and random. But in this case myth rose up from the poem like mist from a river: Here was Ceres. There was Persephone. But the ending was not what was promised. The spring was blighted. And the summer never happened.

"Frühling 1946" forced me to reflect on language, on poetry. I had always seen the myth of Ceres and Persephone as a powerful sign of redemption. But any such understanding was wrenched away by this poem: and I came to think this was not a loss. In fact, it was high time my sense of it was unsettled. In any case, when a myth is stripped of meaning, it simply grows another skin. I had known the myth since I was a child. I had followed it as a poet. But I could never have foreseen that Persephone would be betrayed by Ceres in the terrible offices of the Gestapo in Berlin in 1942. But now that I think of it, the underworld is with us all the time. That is the nature of myth. That is the need for translation. I should have known.

Domestic Violence

During the 1970s I lived in a suburb south of Dublin. The windows of our house looked to the hills. We were in an incline, in the shelter of a small neighborhood. Travelers from all over Ireland had once stopped there to take a well-advertised goat's milk cure.

To the east was the coast. If we pointed the car in that direction we could drive onto the crackling surface of Sandymount Strand. There Stephen Dedalus walks and broods at the start of *Ulysses*; there he says, "History is a nightmare from which I am trying to awake." To the south were the roads which wandered to the interior—Meath, Waterford, Kilkenny. To the north were other roads. They traveled ninety miles, all the way to Belfast. The physical journey was short; the imaginative one was infinite.

Our house was part of the new expansion of the city. All by themselves, these suburbs signaled a new Ireland. The previous decades had been hard-pressed and introverted. Now here at last was the outward-looking place which had been promised: American books and French wines. Cars, fragrances. They crept to the edge of the old nation. They beckoned and enticed.

We were southerners, citizens of the Republic. Belfast was a city over which the Union Jack still flew. In the final year of the sixties, a rift between the Northern Irish communities became an abyss. With every month, the North spiraled deeper into violence. The bombings, sniper fire and internments were confined, with few exceptions, to the counties at the top of the island. But the other violence—cultural, political—spilled out and began to stain the whole country.

A place, a moment. It is the late 1970s. I am up at 7 a.m. I have small children. The morning is chilly. I am in the kitchen, looking out my window at a suburban back garden. For the first five minutes, as I turn on the kettle, watch it steam, pour coffee, I can stare at it uninterrupted.

Then I turn on the radio. Guns and armaments fill the kitchen. Hoods, handcuffs, ArmaLites—the paraphernalia of urban struggle slides easily in and out of the newsreader's voice. A blackbird flickers down into the grass. I can see neighbors' rooftops. The voice continues. An odd thought forms in my mind, painful and inexact. I look around the kitchen, lost in contradictions. Then I realize what it is. My coffee is the instant variety, closed in a glass jar made in Huddersfield. My marmalade comes from London. My kettle from Holland. My knife from Germany. My radio from Japan. Only the violence, it seems—only that—is truly Irish.

And yet this piece is not about war or conflict. It is about a poem. I want to attempt a small biography of a genre. I want to revisit, in the later part of my writing life, what bewildered me in an earlier one. I want to uncover a labyrinth of references whose turns and twists lead not to Irish history, but to my own. I want to explore a counter-history. In other words, the so-called domestic poem.

This poem touched the place I lived and was touched by it. I want to argue here for its scope and reach; for its powerful roots in the unseen world it is accused of denying. I want to map the revealing and interesting resistances to it, which are clues to a course poetry set for itself in modern times.

As someone drawn to the domestic poem, I only slowly became aware of the shadow hanging over it. Gradually I realized it had been designated a lesser genre; almost a sub-genre. In fact, in the nineteenth century the domestic poem was a code for something a poetess was likely to write. A short, soft lyric of unearned sentiment. The four-stress, eight-beat line of an obedient music. Those suspicions lingered well into the twentieth century. "The temptation to decorate is great where the theme may be of the slightest," wrote Virginia Woolf.

Worse still, the domestic poem was connected with corrupt feeling as well as with women poets. Neither association was a benefit. "In the nineteenth century," writes Annie Finch, "the term 'poetess' was typically a conventional compliment to, or acknowledgement of, any female poet's femininity. During the twentieth century it became more often a label of contempt and condescension."

And there is more. This is, after all, a personal piece. I was an Irish woman poet in a bardic culture. The political poem and the public one had been twined together in Ireland since the nineteenth century. There was little dialogue with the domestic. My growing belief—that there was a distance between history and the past in Ireland—was strengthened by that disconnect. History was the official version; the past was an archive of silences.

Already I was interested in a sort of poem which did not

simply look towards a public world, even as compelling a one as the Irish version. The surface of a drinking glass, the shadow of a tree beside a suburban drive—there seemed to be no vocabulary for these things. In contrast, there was an established lexicon for the public poem. The problem was arranging their co-existence.

But it was more than that. The domestic poem, traditionally barred from the public world, confined to a set script, had been drained of meaning. Yet the meanings were there for the taking. The elements of that poem—intimate, uneasy, charged with a relation which is continuous and unpredictable between bodies and the spaces they inhabit—seemed perfectly set up to register an unwritten past. It was an opportunity for Irish poetry. And yet there was no welcome for it anywhere that I could see.

The violence in the North began in the year of our marriage. 1969. The television showed marches, meetings. Then cracked heads. Then gunfire. Then we went to live in the suburb. It was a ragged pattern in my mind. We moved into our new house, the radio always on, the television telling us that nothing would be the same again.

We were young, in our twenties. We were provincials of a country on the edge of violent change. We couldn't see it; we saw our lives, only that. The country was sundered; we were newly joined. At night, in our new house, we sat and listened. We heard the eerie quiet. The thrashing of the chestnuts and sycamores across the road in the wind from the foothills. We heard whispers of our future: cars pulling up and backing out of drives. A last call for a child to come indoors.

And we quarreled. It is what young, newly married people do. We loved each other and we quarreled. And quarreled. Now, after more than thirty-five years of a close marriage, I try to remember. What was it all about? Our voices—or was it just my voice—high and aggrieved; reproaching, accusing. What was I saying? What was I asking? I forget the details. It was the music of our new life. Or part of it.

But I remembered the fact of it. Increasingly, I was haunted by it. Our children were born. The struggle of wills died. But the memory of that young couple in their new house remained. Their raised voices filling the spaces. The back-echo of new rooms. As time went on, memory changed them. They were no longer an isolated pair in a remote suburb. My mind gilded them with significance. I saw them there, young and infuriated. Above all, I sensed their angry words were connected— by a series of inferences, like an underground tunnel—to the larger quarrel happening on the island they inhabited.

What was it I kept going back to? It was more than their youth and anger. It was a puzzle of art rather than life: a split vision. Each time, I returned to them in memory and with design. I remembered the actual setting: unvarnished floors, a small television. But I also thought of what was outside the windows, the sparse trees and disturbed earth of a new suburb. And beyond that again, a troubled, scarred island.

For a poem to convey any of that, it would have to convey all of it. But there was a problem. The domestic poem had a foreground, not a background. There was no depth of field. It was a poem taken from the nineteenth century, which had granted it only one dimension—and that grudgingly. It was not inclusive.

Yet in my mind, at the edge of my page, I sensed connections. A young couple; an afflicted island. The language spoken and unspoken. The private compact of union; the public one of dissension. It was not an abstraction. These were our lives. And yet how could I prove this connection where it needed to be proved—that is, in the poem? How could I show the link between the private and the public when the private side of the equation—that front room—belonged to a world of mundane interiors poetry itself had slighted?

In those moments, I knew I wanted to re-interpret the domestic poem. In my house, on a day with tasks and small children, I felt its about-to-be power everywhere. As a painter's daughter I had memories of my mother arranging flowers, fruit; getting them ready for a still life. I wanted the opposite: to feel that those atoms and planes could be thrown into a fever of spatial dissent; that they moved, re-arranged themselves, threw off their given shapes. I thought of that as the starting point for my poems. When I came on a line of poetry that recognized the terrain, I was moved, as in Elaine Feinstein's powerful last line to her poem "Email from Wellington (unsent)": *You were always home to me. I long for home.*

But how to explore this? And what would that exploration cost? As an Irish poet, the public world of my country—listened to with horror on morning radio—had a claim on my imagination. But if I wrote this so-called domestic poem, would I be banished to a region of private reference? Would the poem I chose—by reason of its form and history—push me away from writing at the center of what was happening to and in my own nation? Had I—like the nineteenth-century woman poet, with her flowers, her religious piety, her timidity—already been assigned a parameter within which I could write? Was it fixed? And if so, who had fixed it?

In those years, surrounded by questions, I thought wistfully of a poem in which the interior and exterior worlds had a new freedom; a symbiotic negotiation, like shadow and light. Edward Hirsch's powerful words apply: ". . . In the practical realm of utility and commerce, poetry is inconsequential, but for the interior world, in the hidden realm of our affective lives, it is curiously deep and renewing. Something that might seem fragile—a group of words arranged on a page—turns out to be indestructible."

I wanted the cut flowers on the table to show the wound of their break with the natural. I wanted the voices of those young people to be heard again. I wanted, imaginatively and figuratively—and only, of course, in the realm of the poem—domestic violence. I knew exactly what I intended by that. I had a deep respect for the customary use of the term to denote a tragic relationship, but I needed the words for a different context, to convey an aesthetic association. The old origins of the word *violence*—taking the Latin word *vis*, or force, and the past participle of *fero*, which is *latus*—means to carry out something through force. I wanted the domestic poem to claim that power. To lift its burden, to bear its freight and to advance. To speak aggressively of reality from its private world. To resemble Job's messenger, coming from a mysterious place, saying *I only am escaped alone to tell thee.*

But how? In a BBC interview in 1962 Sylvia Plath noted it. "I feel that in a novel, for example, you can get in toothbrushes and all the paraphernalia that one finds in daily life, and I find this more difficult in poetry. Poetry, I feel, is a tyrannical discipline, you've got to go so far, so fast, in such a small space that you've just got to turn away all the peripherals. And I miss them! I'm a woman, I like my little Lares and Penates."

I missed them too. But where had it happened? When had poetry made that troublesome investment in separating the ordinary world—the small universe of the cup, the open door, the room—from the epic world of violence and civil struggle?

Occasionally in those years I went to the National Gallery

in Dublin. Often I stopped in front of this or that painting. Always of an interior: A woman's checked dress. A table with a cup on it. After a while watching the painting, these would become my skirt, my cup left on the kitchen counter that very morning. I would hesitate in front of one painting in particular. It was of a room reaching back into the shadow of a corridor—the door open, inviting. If I followed those shadows what would I find?

It was more than curiosity. It was also yearning. I understood that this painterly chronicling of interiors did two things. It documented a space. But it also spoke for it: for its ferocious importance in the lives of those who lived there. It rolled back the boundaries of spatial meaning and revealed the intimacy of the attachment between the body and its immediate horizon. It said that this attachment doesn't only happen when nature instructs the soul, or art elevates the mind. But when a table is laid, a skirt folded, a door opened into an ordinary evening. It left me—as almost everything did at that time—with questions. What made painting capable of that narrative? And not poetry?

Then I was thirty. Then I was thirty-five. When I read poetry now I noticed something I had never seen in my twenties. An absence. I began to register how few *interiors* there were in the poems of the nineteenth and twentieth centuries. There were cities, bridges, meadows, machines, even skylines. But not interiors. Not, that is, the interiors in which people actually lived.

The more I thought about it, the stranger it seemed. There were a few references, certainly. In "Tears, Idle Tears" Tennyson mentions windows. In "The Eve of St. Agnes" Keats constructs a gorgeous, improbable interior. But there is no suggestion that anyone actually lives there. These are theatrical props. In Dickinson there are doors and in one poem, tantalizingly, the cupboard into which she's shut. In Frost, where I looked harder and more expectantly, there are some interiors—but he was a poet who mainly loved to furnish the exterior world.

What made it stranger was that the parallel worlds of fiction and painting were gathering, crowding, pushing those very interiors to the center of the action. Charlotte Brontë doesn't hesitate to describe the "dark coarse drapery" in *Jane Eyre*. Mr. Pecksniff is forthright and unconsciously funny in *Martin Chuzzlewit*: "My daughters' room. A poor first-floor to us, but a bower to them. Very neat. Very airy. Plants you observe; hyacinths; books again; birds," he says. "Such trifles as girls love are here. Nothing more. Those who seek heartless splendor, would seek here in vain."

These are more than references to walls and floors. A whole vista of nuance is here. By now we had had Austen's muslins and dressing tables. George Eliot had shown no difficulty matching "the stony dining room" in *Scenes of Clerical Life* with the weather outside. Elizabeth Gaskell made sure to show the reader the windows "broken and stuffed with rags" in *Mary Barton*. And Trollope's and Thackeray's interiors were about to come into existence. These were fiction writers who had come inside. They were comfortable there. They knew something was happening there which they could not ignore.

When poetry, on the other hand, relents and comes indoors in that era, it is to a posed world. Worse still, having lost its access to interiors, it had gradually lost a language for them. The poem's ability to speak of domestic spaces, and, by inference, of the lives lived in them, was becoming atrophied. A whole teeming world was going on, leaning forward into a future poetry would not share: Time was passing and sofas were becoming couches. Swan-necked pitchers and bowls were turning into basins. Streaming water now came from taps. Food was growing simpler, plates were getting smaller. Plants were being excluded from living rooms and more light was allowed in at windows. Lives changed. The rooms they happened in changed. Poetry remained aloof.

The poetic past is a strange terrain—more inner space than outer. It is a fluid mix of echoes, revelations, set-in-stone critiques and written-in-water poems. Like any poet, I was willing to have an experimental present. The problems came in trying to combine that with an exemplary past.

The first place, the natural place to look, was the Irish nineteenth century. But there was no help there. From 1850 to the end of the century—even where the poems were written by women—it was an asymmetric inventory of political poems.

In almost every case, domestic references were overwhelmed by national ones. Speranza—Lady Jane Wilde, Oscar Wilde's mother—was typical. Her oval, composed face stared back at me out of the lithograph on the frontispiece of her 1871 volume *Poems*. She published her work in Dublin, writing in the house on Merrion Square where she lived with her fashionable doctor husband, Sir William Wilde.

I knew those rooms. I knew their high ceilings, windows blind with light on winter mornings, their lack of heat and eerie acoustics. I had stayed in them. I had visited them. I could see her writing there. But it was no good looking in her poems for a description of them. The details, the exactitude of the interior had been bleached out. All you could find was rhetoric. Her opening poem, "To Ireland," was enough: *My*

country wounded to the heart / Could I but flash along thy soul.
The alternate space I was looking for was plainly not there.

And so I did what many poets have done. I began to look
for those poems and poets which pointed forward to where I
was now. Three in particular struck me, coming at early and
later stages of my reading. I offer them here:

One day, reading a volume of poetry published in 1920, I
stumbled on something. Not an answer, but a hint. It was a
poem about rooms. Not smooth, and not perfect. There was
an awkwardness about it. A cartoon stroke here and there.
Nevertheless, something held and surprised me. It was called,
appropriately, "Rooms":

> *I remember rooms that have had their part*
> *In the steady slowing down of the heart.*
> *The room in Paris, the room at Geneva,*
> *The little damp room with the seaweed smell,*
> *And that ceaseless maddening sound of the tide.*

The cadences were rough yet I felt an energy. What caught
my attention was not the description, but the fact that a poet
was trying to describe a reach and darkness of feeling; and yet
for once placing it inside and not outside. This was not the
domestic poem of the nineteenth century. There were no pre-
set decorums. The argument was opposite: something had
happened in these spaces. Love had died there. Fear was felt
there. Death was coming.

The poem was written by Charlotte Mew. She was born in
London in 1869 to a family tormented by class and conflict:
her father, Fred Mew, was an unqualified architect's assistant,
her mother was the daughter of his employer. There were
seven children, little money and much grief. Three sons died

in childhood. There was an endless scramble to make do: turned collars and darned sleeves.

With adulthood, the real problems began. Her only brother became schizophrenic, soon followed by a much-loved younger sister. Her father died, leaving no money. Her mother, with a tiny inheritance, kept her and her sister alive, in a drifting lifeboat of gentility. Mew published articles, made little money, lived as a recluse, and by the first decade of the twentieth century was a strange, eccentric figure.

And here the story is taken up by Alida Monro. In 1915 Mew was invited to the Poetry Bookshop on the Strand, owned by Monro's husband. Through the door came a tiny, odd woman, not more than four foot ten inches. "Her face was a fine oval," writes Monro in her memoir, "and she always wore a little, hard pork-pie hat put on very straight." Mew was nearly fifty when her first book, *The Farmer's Bride*, was published by Harold Monro's press. She lived for only twelve more years. In the spring of 1928, after the death of her sister, she purchased a bottle of Lysol—a creosote mixture—and drank a glass of it. She died a few hours later.

Only a poet of Mew's ilk, so dissident, so lost, so out on a margin of voice, craft and canon—with so little to gain from poetic convention—could prove a category like the nineteenth-century domestic poem so deficient. Her interiors are re-born subjects for the poem. They are real and surreal. There are chairs, bedrooms, windows in her work. Her interiors are places of force, flexing their power against the outdoors; insisting on being named in the same breath. One of the real unshacklings of the domestic poem begins here.

The second poem I read much earlier. It came from a volume called *Another September*, published in 1958 by a then young Irish poet, Thomas Kinsella. I read it when I was scarcely out of my teens, my ears and eyes still dazed by Yeatsian rhetoric. This hardly seemed from the same tradition. In a way it wasn't.

To start with, the setting of the poem is a "country bedroom." A bedroom, moreover, located in the new Ireland, where downright working lives were lived. The Ireland Seán Ó'Faoláin once referred to as "the grocer's republic." And since the hinterland of this poem is a nation of plain lives, it goes without saying that the rhetoric of the Irish Revival is nowhere to be seen. When the poem opens, there is only silence and ordinary existence. A husband and wife have fallen asleep. It is a dawn at the edge of autumn. Nothing more. Nothing less.

> Dreams fled away, this country bedroom, raw
> With the touch of the dawn, wrapped in a minor peace,
> Hears through an open window the garden draw
> Long pitch black breaths, lay bare its apple trees,
> Ripe pear trees, brambles, windfall-sweetened soil,
> Exhale rough sweetness against the starry slates.
> Nearer the river sleeps St. John's, all toil
> Locked fast inside a dream with iron gates.

My first reading of the poem, many years ago, was lost in the shock of the familiar. *I know this room*, I said to myself. It was not a literary critique but a visceral reaction. I recognized the simple temper and ordinary dimensions of the space. The Irish bedrooms of that era—so many of them built at the back of a house—were the bedrooms of my early childhood. Sparsely furnished; short on luxuries. Their opulence lay in the fact that, more often than not, they looked to the south-facing gardens of a temperate climate—to sweet grass and bird-pecked fruit trees.

But, reading the poem again, something was different. In the paintings I looked at so wistfully in the National Gallery there was often such an intensity of visual effect that the interior itself ceased to be a mere witness and became a participant. Now here was a room which was an actual character in a poem. The bedroom, raw with dawn, wrapped in peace, listens: *Hears through an open window the garden draw / Long pitch black breaths.*

The final two stanzas of the poem—it is relatively short— achieve a transformation. In this context, the interior, as a poetic figure, encompasses what I mean by domestic violence: an intense moral and imaginative upheaval of the kind associated with external revelation in the poetic tradition, but here happening in a domestic space.

> *Domestic Autumn, like an animal*
> *Long used to handling by those countrymen,*
> *Rubs her kind hide against the bedroom wall*
> *Sensing a fragrant child come back again*
> *—Not this half-tolerated consciousness*
> *That plants its grammar in her yielding weather*
> *But that unspeaking daughter, growing less*
> *Familiar where we fell asleep together.*
>
> *Wakeful moth wings blunder near a chair,*
> *Toss their light shell at the glass, and go*
> *To inhabit the living starlight. Stranded hair*
> *Stirs on still linen. It is as though*
> *The black breathing that billows her sleep, her name,*

Drugged under judgment, waned and—bearing daggers
And balances—down the lampless darkness they came,
Moving like women: Justice, Truth, such figures.

The power of the poem, its action and surprise, lies in the last stanza. "The living starlight" receives the moths. But inside the room, it is the "stranded hair" of a sleeping woman that signals visionary change. From the plain sight of a woman asleep arise the mythic figures of Truth and Justice "moving like women."

In the Irish poem, as I understood it, this was new. The locale of the pastoral had been suddenly and unceremoniously shifted. It was as though someone had pushed the background away between scenes in a local theater. A real place is inferred. A place of waking and sleeping. A domestic scene where everything is human and from which the demigods of the pastoral are banished.

Despite the close, even cluttered rhyme scheme, the metrical march of the lines, there is something quirky and conversational here; a voice rehearsing its new freedoms. Later I would read the poem again and hear that voice in the service of argument, image and large intent. The largeness lay in something the domestic poem could establish supremely well: a tense, combative conversation with poetic convention. A poem talking back to pastoral and elegy.

When I read it more closely years later, looking at it in the light of my own unrest, I realized its originality, its sweet-natured dissent all the more. Had it been a conventional nature poem, revelation would have come from the garden—from earth, nurture, renewal. Instead the nature poem, which had waited imperiously for centuries for the poet to come out of doors, to make an obeisance to moral instruction and instructive landscape, has to enter a country bedroom. Has to change its colors and its tune. Has to speak the vernacular of an ordinary life. Has to say the words *love* and *vision* in plain speech.

The final poem confirms these points—not as an English-language poem, but as an instance of the place the domestic poem meets the public one, so that both can be renewed.

In 1943, a German Jewish poet died in Palestine. Her name was Else Lasker-Schüler. Today she is a defining figure of German expressionism, a fascinating dissident. Then, she was a lonely and broken woman.

Lasker-Schüler was born in 1869 in Elberfield in Westphalia. By her middle twenties she had married, had moved to Berlin and became a noted figure there. She published poems and plays. In 1913 an acclaimed volume, *Hebräische Balladen*, came out.

The city of Berlin was hospitable to wayward artists. She dressed as Prince Yussuf and a Dada artist remembers her at a poetry reading in 1914: "Suddenly the lights went out, and Else Lasker-Schüler stepped out onto the stage. She wore a robe made of blue silk. Loose-fitting trousers, silver shoes, a kind of baggy jacket, her hair was like silk, pitch black. But her words were hard, crystal clear. They glowed like metal."

Lasker-Schüler's final years were desolate. She fled the Nazis in the early thirties and lived in Jerusalem. Unlike many other poets who had chosen to live there, she still wrote in her native German. In every sense, she had lost her world. The Israeli writer Yael Lotan was a child then but she remembers her as one of the strange figures in that locale: "There were many such people in Jerusalem in those days, people living a private dream superimposed upon the reality of our city and life . . . She [Else Lasker-Schüler] was a familiar figure on the streets and in the cafes of Jerusalem—tattered and bedizened like a bag-lady, her frail figure bent double. But her eyes still blazed with a black flame and she fed stray cats and dogs when she herself was starving."

There is a painting of Lasker-Schüler, done in 1942, shortly before her death, in which she is looking in the mirror. In it, she has a mask, but also a heavy fur collar in that unlikely climate. Another painting by Ephraim Marcus has a title which describes her plight in those years—*Helpless in an Alien World.*

In 1950 Heinz Politzer, in an article in *Commentary*, left a poignant account of her death and funeral. In her last years, he says, she was "a broken old woman who looked like a solitary exotic nightbird, with enormous eyes in an ageless face." And again: "The Sextons busied themselves with a little bundle smaller than the body of a child."

In 1943, Lasker-Schüler published a final volume of poems. The title poem is called "Mein blaues Klavier" (My Blue Piano). It invokes a world of elegy, of restrained lament. But it is also the exemplary model of a poem in which the boundaries between the domestic and political are made fluid again.

My Blue Piano

At home I have a blue piano.
But I can't play a note.

It's been in the shadow of the cellar door
Ever since the world went rotten.

Four starry hands play harmonies.
The Woman in the Moon sang in her boat.
Now only rats dance to the clanks.

The keyboard is in bits.
I weep for what is blue. Is dead.

Sweet angels I have eaten
Such bitter bread. Push open
The door of heaven. For me, for now—

Although I am still alive—
Although it is not allowed.

In the poem, the piano trembles between the actual and possible, between the lost and recoverable. Put together with the unstable edges of the world it describes, as well as the color blue, it manages to be both surreal and true: a familiar household object and an image of loss. The private world is entrusted to a domestic horizon. This is the piano that was played in a room, in a home. Now it carries extraordinary freight.

As the poem goes on it becomes bolder and stranger. The music is gone. There are rats, there are angels. There is an ominous hinterland of a rotten world. But once again, it is accomplished in an indoors that manages to be both literal and magical, with the memory of an ordinary past blurred into a present made no less desolate by being improbable.

These poems did more than please and console me. I valued them because they resisted an inheritance of perspective I found oppressive: the corrosive effect and tradition of the sublime.

The history of the sublime—enclosing and elusive—has played a central part in poetry. Although the idea may be as old as Longinus, its true moment was the Romantic one. Sixty years before Wordsworth, the eighteenth-century British critic John Baillie wrote of it in this definition: "Vast Objects occasion vast Sensations and vast Sensations give the Mind a higher Idea of her own Powers."

In Edmund Burke's *Philosophical Enquiry into the Origin of our ideas of the Sublime and the Beautiful*, written twenty years later in 1757, Burke re-defined the sublime as what appeared greater than us, what we therefore feared and were awestruck by—whether in landscape or literature.

These ideas challenged the inner world of man to equal the outer one. Challenged sensibility and imagination to construct an inner lexicon which reflected the grandeur of outward landscapes. The idea of grandeur, both in language and landscape, began to change the scale of the poem and the ambitions of the poet. Example, illumination, imitation— these were all characteristic modes of the sublime. "Lives of great men all remind us," wrote Longfellow, "we can make our lives sublime." The scale of the poem and the ambitions of the poet shifted. Modesty was no longer a virtue.

And for poetry, there was some gain—at least in part. The critic Thomas Weiskel tells us that "the sublime revives as God withdraws from an immediate participation in the experience of man." As poetry lost its arts of magic, and then its place on the right side of religion, something had to replace it. Hence the sublime.

But for me, when I was a young woman, the sublime was not abstract history: it was a grandiose and off-putting instruction set. A cumbersome warning of how unimportant the ordinary life could be. It was the dark alter ego of my wishes, my ambitions. I woke up in a modest, contemporary suburb in Ireland. The curtains drew back on the ordinary. Light fell on the blue cup. The saucer began its slow continual turn. A child opened its mouth. A tree lost a leaf. Not one of these small events challenged the inner world of man or woman to equal the outer one. Not one of them met the prescriptions of the sublime. Quite the opposite. They invited accuracy, not grandeur. Precision, not scale.

Can any one poet say poetry was wrong? Can a single writer challenge a collective past? My answer is simple. Not only can, but should. Poetry should be scrubbed, abraded, cleared, and re-stated with the old wash stones of argument and resistance. It should happen every generation. Every half-generation. In every working poet's life and practice.

As a young poet I stepped back from aesthetics. It was the era of the New Criticism, of modernism, of ordained poetic authority. The critique of the poem, shadowed and strengthened by sciences of reason and textual analysis, seemed powerful but also alien. Only gradually did I begin to realize that this was beside the point: that every poet has to make their own critique. That authority inheres in that; and only that.

It was easier said than done. The problem is that no young poet goes from theory to practice. Always the other way round. Like so many other young poets, my practice was self-doubting and so my theory was unlikely to be confident. All the same, I was noting things, taking them in, waiting for a day I could be sure.

A poem is a subtle system of references. It codifies, suggests, infers. It gestures outward while staring obdurately inward. Looked at closely, it can tell you about a society. Looked at from a distance, it can reveal a history of evasion. Only later, armed with my own questions, did I feel comfortable enough to challenge some inherited ideas. This essay records those questions. Most of all, I took courage from other poets' questions and answers—often American poets. I heard the clear voice of Adrienne Rich: "Who is to dictate what may be written about and how? Isn't that what everybody fears—the prescriptive, the demand that we write out of certain materials, avoid others?" And Allen Ginsberg: "Poetry is not an expression of the party line. It's that time of night, lying in bed, thinking what you really think, making the private world public, that's what the poet does."

Finally, I made my own questions. Perhaps, as poets, that is all we really have for a critique: an endless, self-renewing series of interrogative thoughts. "The historical sense," wrote T. S. Eliot, "involves a perception, not only of the pastness of the past, but of its presence." How had it happened that poetry's historical sense only came alive when it left the house? What did it mean for generation after generation of poets that the world outside was deemed to be a horizon of moral transcendence and pastoral significance? But not a half-empty cup, a child's shoe, a crooked patch of sunlight on carpet?

Finally, I learned to listen for the confirming words of other poets. As for instance these: In a 1999 interview, Philip Levine spoke of Antonio Machado in these terms: "He's able to transform all these essentially simple things into a kind of wholeness and holiness. And it seemed to me that Machado was able to validate these very basic experiences that we all share—and that we begin to think of, in our busy lives, as marginal. But Machado brings them into the center of his experience and his poetry. And I thought, *Oh, what genius that was, to take what we've marginalized and pull it into the center and make it what sheds light on everything else.*"

Maps

Adrienne Rich

When I first read Adrienne Rich's poems I was in my early thirties. I was married with small children. I was far away from some of the claimed ground in her work and not yet sure of my own. Hers are, after all, American poems, written from the heart of the American empire as a century darkens. They are fiercely questioning, deeply political, continuously subversive. They celebrate the lives of women; the sexual and comradely love between them. They contest the structure of the poetic tradition. They interrogate language itself. In all of this, they describe a struggle and record a moment which was not my struggle and would never be my moment. Nor my country, nor my companionship. Nor even my aesthetic.

And yet these poems came to the very edge of the rooms I worked in, dreamed in, listened for a child's cry in. They passed through the frost of a suburban dark, the early light of a neighborhood summer. I took whichever book they were happening in from place to place, propping it against jars and leaving it after me on chairs and beside coffee cups. Even as I did so, I felt that the life I lived was not the one these poems commended. It was too far from the tumult, too deep in the past. And yet these poems helped me live it.

How could they? There is something about the way a strong poet speaks that is radical in the literal sense of the word: uprooting both chronology and the need for similarity. In the process, the reader can be strengthened. I can give just one example. I remember a conference in London in the early eighties. My children were small; it was an effort to be there. The conference itself, on women's writing, was exciting and exhausting. At night, in my hotel room, it was hardly quieter. It was late spring; rain was falling. The big, cumbersome buses braked hard. Tires hissed all night through the borough of Kensington.

Gradually I shut it out with the book I was reading, *The Dream of a Common Language*, published five or six years earlier. One poem in particular I stayed with: "From an Old House in America." The house in question was in Vermont, a place I had never seen. The landscape was unfamiliar. The lines were short, fused into plangent couplets, describing things I didn't know and would probably never encounter. Yet through their agency, another home solidified on the page: open to weather, dark with elegy. A house glowing with danger as well as memory. A house with lost objects that kept finding a past: a pack of playing cards, a red truck, dried-out watercolor paints— all of them summarized in the luminous phrase "the humble tenacity of things."

And with those words on the page, despite the distractions of traffic and distance, I could find my own house in Dublin on another road, south of another city. At dusk there the windows made a yellow line—a signature of teatime reunions, of secrets, of small perseverances. Its light was different; its meaning still unfinished. And yet I felt both it and myself given shelter in the melody and regret of the poem I was reading. Years later, I would remember my exact sense of this when I read a sentence from Adrienne Rich's acceptance speech at an awards ceremony. *I am both a poet and one of the everybodies of my country.*

As they permeated the small barriers of place and distraction, these poems also began to open my mind to new ideas of who writes a poem and why. A truly important poet changes two things, and never one without the other: the interior of the poem and external perceptions of the identity of the poet. By so doing, they prove that the two are inextricable. That these radicalisms not only connect, they actually have their source in each other. After the poem is changed in front of us, after our conservatisms are unwritten by a marvelous cadence or a surprising leap from stanza to stanza, only then do we look up, suddenly ready to see that only someone with a new sense of the poet's life and authority could have done this. But if these poems achieve—and I believe they do—this degree of innovation, they are also rooted deep in a human life. And that perhaps is the place to begin.

ADRIENNE RICH was born in Baltimore, Maryland, in the early summer of 1929. Her father was a pathologist at Johns Hopkins University and Jewish. Her mother was Southern and Gentile. One of her early poems, "At the Jewish New Year," states, *Whatever we strain to forget / Our memory must be long.* Her background was never entirely cast off. On the contrary, the tension between male and female, between historic pride and vulnerable identity has become one of the charged centers of her work.

In 1951 she graduated from Radcliffe College. Within eight years she had received a Guggenheim Fellowship, published two volumes of poetry, had married and given birth to three sons. Somewhere in the middle of all this we get a glimpse of her one rainy night in Massachusetts: a poignant eyewitness account.

"Short black hair, great sparkling black eyes and a tulip-red umbrella: honest, frank, forthright and even opinionated." Sylvia Plath's impression of Adrienne Rich, recorded in this sentence in her journals, marks their first meeting. The year was 1958. Adrienne Rich was twenty-nine. The comment catches a woman who was still young, still not quite free of her moorings.

In one sense, how could she be? The American mid-century was an exciting place for a young woman poet to be, provided she looked, and continued to look, as if she would cause no trouble. An example is W. H. Auden's selection of her first volume, *A Change of World*, for the Yale Younger Poets Award. What the selection gave with one hand, the citation took away with the other. In an odd choice of words, he assigned to the poems little more than the virtues of a Victorian childhood.

"The poems a reader will encounter in this book," he wrote in his preface, "are neatly and modestly dressed, speak quietly but do not mumble, respect their elders but are not cowed by them and do not tell fibs." Albert Gelpi, who with Barbara Charlesworth Gelpi has edited the essential Norton Critical Edition on Rich's work, says of this comment: "In other words the stereotype—prim, fussy, schoolmarmish—

that has corseted and strait-laced women poets into "poetesses" whom men could deprecate with admiration."

Adrienne Rich's first two books, *A Change of World*, published in 1951, and *The Diamond Cutters and Other Poems* from 1955, were restrained and eloquent. The poems are elegantly crafted: the voice is distinct but muted. In one of them, "Storm Warnings," she writes, *These are the things that we have learned to do / Who live in troubled regions.* But a real storm warning does not occur until her third book, *Snapshots of a Daughter-in-Law: Poems 1954–1962*, whose title poem was a liberation.

"Snapshots of a Daughter-in-Law" is a threshold poem. Suddenly the lines are longer. The voice is clear, fractious and definite: *A thinking woman sleeps with monsters.* Here for the first time we catch sight of the mid-century heroine: a woman who shaves her legs until they gleam like petrified mammoth-tusk, who imagines Emily Dickinson in her Amherst parlor while the jellies boil and scum. For the first time, we hear a distinctive note: the sound of a silenced woman suddenly able to voice a conventional suppression in terms of an imaginative one.

"It was an extraordinary relief to write that poem," states Rich in her essay "When We Dead Awaken." The early containment of images and line lengths was now over. "In those years," she wrote in the same essay, "formalism was part of the strategy—like asbestos gloves it allowed me to handle materials I couldn't pick up barehanded."

From this point the work changed, deepened, strengthened. Between 1964 to 1971 Rich published three books. *Necessities of Life: Poems 1962–1965. Leaflets: Poems 1965–1968* and *The Will to Change: Poems 1968–1970.* The themes were various, but the signal was clear. The poems would not stay on the page.

They were out in the world. They were deep in negotiation with the political climate of the day mediated through Rich's changing sense of her life and the American ethos.

During these years she moved to New York City with her family. She began to teach in open admissions at City College of New York. She was active against the Vietnam War and increasingly involved in the women's movement. Her father died. Her husband died. By 1974 when *Diving into the Wreck*—a cornerstone volume—was published, she had made a powerful and seamless integration of her various lives as mother, lesbian, activist and poet.

Many of the poems that mark this growth and change still have an extraordinary resonance. "Orion" from *Leaflets* for instance, with its glittering, androgynous prince of the night sky, who may well lend some of his elemental grace and endurance to the mysterious swimmer of "Diving into the Wreck." And "Planetarium," where the emphasis is not on discovery, but the discoverer: a woman astronomer, opening up the power of the skies through the nature of her body.

These poems established a forward movement which was continued in *The Dream of a Common Language* (1978), *A Wild Patience Has Taken Me This Far* (1981), *Your Native Land, Your Life* (1986) and *Time's Power* (1989). These in turn were followed by the important volume, *An Atlas of the Difficult World* (1991), and the lovely, overcast lyricism of a more recent book, *Dark Fields of the Republic*.

Space allows only a few signposts. Nevertheless "Power," "North American Time," "For Memory" and Section XIII of "An Atlas of the Difficult World" as well as "Diving into the Wreck" itself and "Six Narratives" are all essential reading. These, with the beautiful love poem which is Section XII of "Twenty-one Love Poems" from *The Dream of a Common Lan-*

guage, show the extent of the terrain in these poems: a horizon leveled over the political and private lands of an adventurous spirit. *I came to explore the wreck.*

WHEN THE READER finishes a chronological selection of Rich's poems, one question may well persist. What exactly happened in the tumultuous distance between a *A Change of World* and *Dark Fields of the Republic*? What transformed the young poet Auden singled out for her good manners into one of the great subversive poets of our time? The customary, and sometimes hostile, critical view is that Adrienne Rich became feminist, activist, lesbian. That her angers cut her adrift from mainstream poetry. That America lost a gifted lyric poet and had to make do with a polemicist.

Sexual choice and political disaffection are certainly central themes in Rich's work. But they are ways of attaching this poet to the world, not repudiating it. The love between women, sexual and ethical, becomes a visionary strategy for imagining a new America: a new order, a different language. It is the irreducible force behind the revelations of love and insistence which energize these poems. Even when that involves— as the line from "Twenty-one Love Poems" suggests—*all the time nursing, measuring that wound.* But Adrienne Rich is also a sophisticated, pilgrim-like traveler in the poetic past as well as the historical one. And in that past, poetry has also been wounded. The fragmentation which she most addresses in her work occurs wherever the moral voice divides from the imagining intelligence.

A number of poems—"Diving into the Wreck" and "Power" and "North American Time" and "For Memory" to name just a few—speak to the injustices of a society. They also speak directly to that invitation to the poet to remain in a private kingdom of music and perception. Whether flying over the speckled light of New York after dark or fathoming a metaphoric underworld, the poet's inference is the same: any menace to human beings constitutes a moral imperative, not just for other men and women, but for poetry itself.

This is a powerful and essential argument: that the ethical vision is a functioning part of the poetic imagination and not an optional addition. For her discovery and command of that vision—and for her insistence on restoring it from the margins to the poetic center—Adrienne Rich is rightly seen as one of the shape-makers of her century's poetry.

I want to finish with a few sentences from the essay I did not write here: the document of Adrienne Rich's influence on me. Women poets have asserted their place in poetry now for several generations. There are now more poems and more poets. The silence is filling up with words. And so there is coming to be, I believe, a shift in the tradition, by which women can not only influence what is handed on, but how it is handed on. Therefore the old codes of example and inheritance, the stern bequeathing of poetic authority—which was once presented as the only way to make a canon—is beginning to change. I like to think that the customs of friendship, as well as the loving esteem which are so visible in the communal life of women, will become evident in the practice and concept of the poetic tradition also. That women poets, from generation to generation, will befriend one another. In that sense I have had Adrienne Rich's friendship. And I could not have done without it.

Elizabeth Bishop:
An Unromantic American

I

American poetry was a rare commodity in the Dublin bookshops of the sixties and seventies. It could turn up, unpredictably and at random, slanted in with books of British verse and Yugoslavian translation, so that the mode of its appearance had an adverse effect on the nature of its readership. Not surprisingly, therefore, my first encounter with Elizabeth Bishop was not in a bookshop at all. I came across her poem "The Moose" in an anthology of American verse I had been sent for review. I read the first stanza. I read the second and marked the place. Later that night, with the children in their cots and the house quiet, I began to read her again.

A Dublin summer night in the suburbs is all dampness and growth. Eleven o'clock marks a turning point: it divides evening from night, the end of one day from the genesis of the next. Television sets are turned off. Cars are driven into garages with an odd, underwater echo. By midnight the only break in the silence is the young dog a few gardens away who starts up at any noise, like a badly rigged alarm.

This sort of night was second nature to me. Every shift and sight in it had a complex familiarity. But as I read Elizabeth Bishop's poem, my night began to give way to the quicker, more magical dark of hers. As I followed her short stanzas, with their skids and recoveries, my sense of place yielded to hers. The turning of mortice locks and the breathing of children was transformed into a terrain of "neat, clapboard churches." The poplars outside became the "hairy, scratchy, splintery" dark of the New Brunswick woods. The Gulf Stream Irish night turned to the "shifting, salty, thin" fog near Bass River. And I was lost in and to the poem.

After that summer night I did what I could to discover more about Elizabeth Bishop's work. I bought her books, studied her poems, tried to unravel the secrets of her prose. None of this was as concerned or conscious as it looks with hindsight. It was gradual and random; yet, once I had read "The Moose," inevitable. It was also difficult. I found it hard to understand the sources of her vision and the necessity for her statement. The process of rapport seemed more flawed and disrupted than with any other poet I had been drawn to. But there were reasons.

II

No poet enters the life and work of another, whatever the disruptions of time and distance, through words alone. Poets imagine each other. They think and think until their own sense of the narrow streets of Florence explains the light and passion of the *Paradiso*. Or the Welsh marshes and the chill of northwest England illuminates *Pearl*. They imagine the cattle train bringing Mandelstam to Smirsk or the freezing room in Devon where Sylvia Plath worked. It is hardly a pure critical process. All the same I feel sure it is in these fires of rapport that poets have found and loved one another for a millennium.

For all that, I had difficulty reconstructing Elizabeth Bishop's life. Part of this was circumstantial. For decades Ireland had been shut off from the American poetic experience. Yeats has described how, as a young poet, he went from place to place with *Leaves of Grass* in his pocket. But he is the exception. In a general sense, the temperate climate in which another poetry could thrive and be understood was missing.

In the sixties all that began to change. American poetry— through journals, articles, imported books—began to come to Ireland. It was an uncertain and frustrating process. A student then at Trinity College in Dublin, I listened eagerly to discussions of American poetry. Wilbur was talked about—this was the mid-sixties. Lowell's *Life Studies* was not yet widely known but his "Quaker Graveyard in Nantucket" was in several British anthologies. ("Hashed-up Melville," one young poet said to me sternly when I admired it.) Sylvia Plath was already dead—this was 1964—and much discussed. "Homage to Mistress Bradstreet" and "Heart's Needle" were talked about as being opposite ends of a virtuoso scale. Elizabeth Bishop was never mentioned.

There are explanations for this, and they amount to more than the vagaries of editors and anthologies. At that time it was the American poets most assimilable to the Yeatsian tradition who found a hearing in Ireland. Poets like Roethke,

Lowell, Berryman looked familiar to an Irish audience. They occupied the center of their own work, as Yeats did with his. They appeared to mediate their world through a controlled and controlling self. However alien their technical freedoms— and I would not want to minimize this—they nevertheless confronted the Irish reader with recognizable and somehow consoling problems. They posed questions about whether the self in their poems was invented or created. They forced the reader to ask how much of their material was manipulated by being mediated through such a self.

Those are ethical and aesthetic questions. *We have been here before*, whispered the Irish reader. *We know this: this is poetry.* But Elizabeth Bishop's work fell outside such questions and answers. At first sight, it was entirely estranged from the patterns and responses of post-war Yeatsian Romantic poetry.

Since a critique of her work was so lacking when I was a young poet I tended to find her in the uncertain ways I have described. Being unsure how or where to place her, I had to rely on illicit, critical methods to understand her: on snatches of comparison, modes of rapport which involved me trawling through my experience to understand hers. If, therefore, in this part of my argument, I seem to be looking for her meaning as an American poet in terms of my own intuitions of Irishness, it's because this was the only way at first I could find access to her work.

III

Her birth, for instance. In Worcester, Massachusetts, in 1911. It is a world away from anything I knew. I was born in the

Dublin of the forties and raised for the first five years of my life under the high ceilings and the cold proportions of a Victorian house near Stephen's Green.

I was the youngest of five. She lost her father when she was eight months old. More tragically, her mother, Gertrude Bulmer Bishop, was institutionalized when she was very young. And yet it's difficult to isolate moments when the full weight and cost of these early losses become apparent in Bishop's work. Only a few poems of hers speak directly about these matters. One of them is the luminous "Sestina": A grandmother and child sit together in a kitchen. The child is drawing a house. The grandmother is making tea. The shadow and chill of a great loss move in and out of the required repetitions of each word: *stove, tears, almanac, house, child, time.*

As each word is repeated, the poem cycles through a sequence of surreal images. The teakettle's "small hard tears" linger for a moment in the real world. But then the tears become buttons on the child's drawing of a man's coat. And the buttons fall down into the flower bed. The almanac talks and the stove whispers its resignation—"it was to be." And now the themes appear more clearly: The child in the kitchen is desolate. The old grandmother cannot replace the stricken mother. In the end, the musical constraint which the sestina places on the theme is a reminder of the constraints which Elizabeth Bishop put on private revelation.

In fact, the most disclosing statements of grief in Elizabeth Bishop's work are also the most ritualized. In "Sestina" and her celebrated villanelle "One Art," she entrusted some of her deepest intuitions of loss to two of the most complex game-forms in poetry. Both poems recall Jeanette Winterson's poignant comment about the effect T. S. Eliot's poetry had on her when she was young: "I still find myself back on the library steps, calm but not tranquilised, freed from my own overwhelming emotion by the poet's contained emotion."

"One Art" was published in *Geography III*, her last book. But there are differences between the two poems. "Sestina" is packed with half-tones and dropped hints. It operates on two levels. Within it a terrible sorrow is happening; is in fact the defining action of the poem. And yet the teakettle keeps boiling, the stove is warm. Only we, outside the poem, piece together the full meaning of it all.

"One Art" is different. "The art of losing isn't hard to master," the poem begins. Then there is a throwaway inventory of what's been lost: a watch, some cities, "a joking gesture." The poem makes full use of the anti-narrative powers of the villanelle. The tone, which is both casual and direct, is deliberately worked against the form in a way it is not in "Sestina." There is a jauntiness about the lost watch, the fable-sized houses that get lost, the continent that can't be found. Once again, Bishop shows that she is best able to display feeling when she can most constrain it.

IV

In 1934 Elizabeth Bishop entered Vassar. Twenty-eight years later I walked into the front square of Trinity College in Dublin. In these circumstances, surely, it would be possible to connect with her. But again there is a lack of correspondence. America in the thirties is a world away from Dublin in the sixties. To start with, the poetic traditions are dissimilar. In her essay on Marianne Moore, "Efforts of Affection," Elizabeth Bishop discusses the older poet as precedent and exemplar.

By the time she came to meet her, "I had already," she writes, "read every poem of Miss Moore's I could find."

When I started to write, Ireland offered no such precedent. There were no Irish women poets I was likely to meet—as Elizabeth Bishop met Marianne Moore—on the bench to the right of the door leading into the reading room of the New York Public Library. There were no visits to a Brooklyn apartment with waist-high bookcases and carpenter's tools hanging by the kitchen. There was nobody I knew—still less a distinguished poet—who would take Mary McCarthy's *The Company She Keeps* to the basement and burn it. It's easy enough now to parody the slightly starchy, genuinely old-fashioned decorum of such a friendship. Their relationship may have been eccentric. But in poetic terms, as far as I was concerned, it was never less than enviable.

Yet I was—if I had only known it—fortunate. I felt the absence of a female poetic precedent. Nevertheless, I was writing within the literary tradition of a defeated people; in a continuum with its own power and freedom. American literature, on the other hand, seemed to explore the relation of its writers to a nation established by history and made visible by event. Irish writers had none of this. They had to invent, improvise, experiment. James Joyce wrote of the "uncreated conscience" of his race; Yeats of the "indomitable Irishry."

Once I began reading them, I could see that American poets had a different point of departure. When Lowell wrote of the Union Dead or Robert Frost asserted, "The land was ours before we were the land's," there was a sense—even allowing for the internal exile of the writer—of an historical consensus.

But Elizabeth Bishop didn't seem to me to have the same national sense as her contemporaries. She didn't seem capable of writing a line like "the pure products of America go crazy," as William Carlos Williams had. Her terms of reference were often geographical rather than historical. She used place as an index of loss; almost never as a measure of identity. The American poets of her generation who addressed the national experience did so in terms of a private and public identity. She remained wryly outside this. "I am green with envy of your kind of assurance," she wrote to Robert Lowell. The remark is revealing and I will come back to it. But for the moment she remained stubbornly in her own private, imaginative territory. The more I read her the more I realized that her obsession—revealed in the cool distances and painful detail of the poems—was with the inability to belong rather than the need to.

Over the years I grew familiar with the archive of feeling stored in Irish literature. I also valued something which Irish literature was rich in: the sense of exile. In some of the best Irish writers, such as Joyce and Beckett, it seemed to be a response to the weight of the past. It made me recall Ellen Bryant Voigt's compelling simile from "Year's End": *like refugees who listen to the sea, / unable to fully rejoice, or fully grieve.*

I saw something similar in Elizabeth Bishop's work. When I thought of her fishhouses, her cold springs, her ability to detail the color of a sky or the shiver of an iris, they seemed an index of exile. I saw that she could relate to places with the precision and surprise of the traveler: the inner émigré, who sees them for the first time and may never see them again.

Looked at closely, Elizabeth Bishop's poetry is full of images of estrangement. But those images can't exist alone. If they do they can only be part of a fractured world, whose lights they may catch but never properly refract. They have to be liberated by an act of poetic coherence. In Larkin and

Yeats—to take two poets in her neighborhood and whom she admired deeply—that coherence is often musical. Yeats relied on metrical structures for the "ice and salt" which he thought were the "best packing" for a poem. In Sylvia Plath the coherence, when it is there, is in the energy of sound as much as anything else. But in Elizabeth Bishop it is always tonal.

V

Poetic tone is more than the speaking voice in which the poem happens; much more. Its roots go deep into the history and sociology of the craft. I imagine that when the early poet-prophets chanted their songs of harvest it was their tone, as much as anything else, that made their audiences listen. *Do not doubt us*, that sound would have said.

Even today, for a poet, tone is not a matter of the aesthetic of any one poem. It grows more surely, and more painfully, from the ethics of the art. Its origins must always be in a suffered world rather than conscious craft. The priest-poets drew their authority from the fear they shared with their listeners: of death, of pestilence, of abandonment by their gods. The modern poet holds only human suffering in common with his audience. He or she draws authority from that. Or fails to have it because of that.

By this reckoning, tone has less to do with the *expression* of a poet's experience than with the *impression* that experience first made. It reveals a poet's choices. It establishes a distance between the poet and their material which is then deflected into the distance between the poem and reader.

Elizabeth Bishop had a rare mastery of tone. It went with her intense commitment to craft. As Alice Quinn said in *Edgar*

Allan Poe & The Juke-Box, her superb study of Bishop's drafts, "Thinking about poetry in the highest terms was instinctive for Bishop and meeting her own standards was almost impossible." Her modulation of voice can seem surprising and even, at times, inappropriate. But this is part of her approach, which is marked by a sort of brilliant, demotic gambling. An example is "At the Fishhouses." It is a longish poem. She uses narrative time to slow down the lyric crescendo. There is a deceptively casual way in which she describes an old man, his purple-brown net in the twilight, the smell of codfish.

Then she begins her superb meditation on water as an emblem of tragic knowledge. Suddenly the water becomes an "element bearable to no mortal." This, you say to yourself, is serious music. It shows poetic intent: an outward element—this almost intolerable water—will be shown, before the poem finishes, to correspond to the interiors of human knowledge. And the life of feeling flinches from both the water and the cold truths it suggests. But then, suddenly, as you read more deeply, the serious emphasis appears to be squandered; thrown away even: A seal shows itself in the water. She sees him. He is, the speaker says, curious and "interested in music." In fact, the speaker is used to singing him Baptist hymns.

What on earth is this? you say. Or out of it, for that matter? Why is this refugee from a bedtime story popping up—and literally—at the center of a metaphysical moment? For a moment or two, you feel certain the poem can't recover its momentum. But it does. The seal disappears. The music returns. The water is back: "Cold dark deep and absolutely clear."

It seems, on first reading, almost an intolerable risk. Almost a reckless intrusion on the poem's movement towards revelation. But of course it's not. By the end of the poem it's obvious that the digression has been a deliberate strategy: an essential strengthening of the abstraction. It's also obvious that what has held the poem together is tone. It acts as a register of Bishop's confidence in the experience she is unfolding. When the seal enters the poem and unsettles us, the tone steadies us. It says, No, wait: this cerebral landscape will only become real when you see how absurd it is to try and humanize its creatures.

To her contemporaries, especially Lowell and Randall Jarrell, Bishop's tone was one of the immediate pleasures of her work. When Jarrell calls her poems "quiet, truthful, sad, funny," he is referring at least in part to the tone in which they happen. But the tone is more than that. It represents and heralds an achievement which occurred at great cost. Robert Pinsky touches on this in his essay "The Idiom of a Self." He infers the dangers of simply regarding her tone as a colloquial melody and her poetry as a painterly triumph: "It is ironic," he writes, "that Bishop is often praised, sometimes faintly, for having a loving eye toward the physical world; it is a matter of her mind, not her eye, and the process is equally as embattled or resistant as it is loving."

These tensions, between surrender and resistance, observation and vision, are held and poised in her tone. There can be, in certain poets, a disparity between voice and tone; an irritating inflation of the voice or an equally unsettling diminution of it *by* the tone. These are always central flaws. They imply a loss of nerve, an uncertainty of poetic conviction.

In Elizabeth Bishop voice and tone are uncannily balanced. An example must be the wonderful moment in "The Moose" when the animal looms up in the woods. The voice in these stanzas is profoundly serious: this is an epiphany, an incarnation of both femininity and instinct. We don't doubt it. The reason we don't is that we receive it through a tone so perfectly judged to the moment: wry, wondering and at peace. The moose is described in affectionate epigrams. It's "homely as a house." It's also "safe as houses." But once again, the final effect is a tonal achievement.

VI

I came to Elizabeth Bishop's work as an Irish poet; an Irish woman poet, at that. I have written of my discovery of her in these terms. I have stayed with this portraiture, allowing huge blanks to build on the canvas—even around the features—because I think it may reveal something of the complex assumptions which a poet from one country brings to the work of a poet from another.

Since it took me years, and many revisions of perspective, before I could connect my Irishness with my womanhood and both with my poetry, I have been drawn, in this context, to a final question. One which, for me, has a central importance. In what sense is Elizabeth Bishop an American poet? The answer is: obliquely. And yet that obliquity seems to be a defining angle of vision.

It goes without saying that her work adds texture and resonance to the tradition of American poetry. But it is more than that. She seems to me to define her country, as so many good Irish writers do, through her estrangement from it. Other skies, other terrains fill her work. She knew that she commented from the edges, from the margins. She seemed to accept that she was an American poet, not a national one.

Yet the wry tone she used in a letter to Robert Lowell about *Life Studies* is quietly subversive. It infers—kindly but with an edge—that types of belonging may well have their source in dangerous self-inflation and self-deception. That naming the past is not quite the same thing as knowing it. "And here I must confess (and I imagine most of your contemporaries would confess the same thing) that I am green with envy of your kind of assurance. I feel I could write in as much detail of my Uncle Artie, say—but what would be the significance?"

Poetic luck can change. Traditions and heritages have a way of altering. Writers who exist on the margins of their age can, with the passage of time and resistance, move to the center of a nation's consciousness. Irish writing is full of examples. By now we are almost used to the fact that certain writers— Joyce and Beckett are examples—can only find their country, or indeed be found by it, through their exile from it.

Elizabeth Bishop was admired by friends and contemporaries. She enjoyed critical acclaim. And yet I am still surprised by the many commentaries of the sixties and early seventies which mention her with respect but as an afterthought. Her hesitation in the face of a ready-made American identity, her refusal of the orthodox stance within the poem—these are qualities which may well have delayed her absorption in those decades into the pantheon of American poetry.

It is now plain—it has been obvious for years—that if she hesitated in her conversation with an American experience which Williams, Lowell and Berryman easily laid claim to, it was because she was involved in delicate and important estrangements from it. For a great part of her working life, she was away from the American mainland. In interviews she spoke of herself as feeling "like a guest."

There is hardly anything so elusive as the way in which a poetic inheritance is sifted and re-arranged from one generation to the next. Any glance at a pile of old anthologies will show how pitiless each generation is in deciding which poets will console and refresh it. From year to year, the sifting goes on, almost invisibly. Poems are read in lonely rooms, in solitary humors, by people for whom the love of poetry is a do-or-die part of their lives. The poem and the reader enter into a mysterious transaction, composed of time and memory and obsession. The mystery of it resides in the fact that—if it is a good poem, or even a great one—the mortal reader will assist it to live on.

I find it immensely poignant that Elizabeth Bishop, who would not make the American experience her private legend, has re-defined the American canon. It must be clear to anyone who has read her work that the complexity of her estrangement will be, from now on, a new and important part of the American myth. Ironically, in her failure to possess it, she has added to it.

Charlotte Mew:
An Introduction

I

Charlotte Mew was born in London in 1869. Her family—middle-class, respectable, afflicted—lived at number 30 Doughty Street in the borough of Camden. I lived near there as a child in the 1950s, when the airy squares with their chestnut and plane trees, their white wedding-cake houses, were still almost intact.

By that time, however, London was pitted and humbled by two wars. To find Charlotte Mew's city we have to peel back the erosion, the doubt, the fog-scars of a hundred years until we come to a place that glows with empire. Pepys's London. The London of the novelists. A few houses down, nearer to Russell Square, Charles Dickens had written his early novels in number 48. What more could a child like Charlotte Mew want, you might ask, than to be born in the environs of a luminous gossip and a great novelist?

The census of April 4, 1881, suggests a normal Victorian family with their children: Henry H. Mew, aged fifteen, "Scholar," Charlotte M. Mew, aged eleven, "Scholar," Caroline F. A. Mew, aged seven, and Freda K. Mew, aged two, together with the live-in servants: Elizabeth Goodman, aged fifty-six, "Nurse Domestic," and Lucy Best, aged eighteen, "Cook Domestic."

But appearances, here as elsewhere, can be deceptive. A more vulnerable and struggling family would be hard to find. The terrible story begins early. One child died. Two more died when Charlotte was seven, one of fever, the other of convulsions. Her only brother, Henry, became schizophrenic early in life. And her youngest sister, Freda, notable in that homely family for being "beautiful as a flame," became schizophrenic at sixteen.

It must all have bewildered Frederick Mew, Charlotte's father. He was an architect, but not a particularly enterprising one. His wife, the daughter of a more eminent architect, had social and financial expectations he failed to fulfill. Fred Mew's income did not increase. But his family did. By 1879 there were seven children. The shadows were growing longer.

Death. Insanity. Class. Suddenly, in that apparent decorum of imperial England, a window opens into a savage time. The Mew family are the dark side of empire. Charlotte Mew lived the pain and contradiction: the shame of a genteel life endured without the money gentility requires; the pain of a sexuality gentility would reject.

II

In 1888 the family moved to Gordon Street. A larger, more expensive and far more unlucky house. Charlotte Mew attended the Gower School. There, within the space of four years, two of the children drifted into insanity. Henry, Charlotte's only brother, was confined to hospital in his early twenties and never re-emerged. His death certificate of March 1901 lists the place of dying as Peckham House Lunatic Asylum. He is said to be buried in Nunhead Cemetery. Freda, the beautiful youngest girl, followed him in her late teens. Alida Monro, a later friend of Mew, opened a small window into the events when she commented: "Their sad condition was a constant torment to Charlotte."

The startling, off-kilter poems published when she was nearly fifty years of age in her first book, *The Farmer's Bride*, gather and mediate the tragedies of Charlotte Mew's youth. They have an eerie verve, these poems. Their conversational staccato, played off against the truncated cadences of Victorian lyric, gives a studio acoustic to the voice. The voice—and this is unusual in that era—signals from its margins and its music through tone. The combination of the two tells us something we can hardly ignore:

> No year has been like this that has just gone by;
> It may be that what Father says is true,
> If things are so it does not matter why:
> But everything is burned and not quite through.

Mew is not a lyric poet. At least, not a conventional one—and certainly not in that era of lyric poets. She is something different and far more unexpected: she is a pre-modernist narrator, gathering her world into lines which tumble off the edge of the page with the strain of holding it together. Cemeteries, asylums, sea roads and broken dolls clutter these lines. The cast of characters is more estranged than strange.

While the Georgian poets of that era were seeking out small pastorals, she marked a disharmony. She stands in the middle of her Edwardian landscape, not to be framed by it, but to signal its danger, like a fire-swallower at an otherwise sedate country fair.

These qualities did not guarantee a literary welcome. Mew received little recognition in her lifetime. The full chill of neglect can be felt in the lines in a local newspaper noticing her death. She is described as "Charlotte New, said to be a writer." She had not even lived safely, to use Deborah Digges's graceful phrase, *inside the brick and mortar of a name.* The earlier years were no better. She was not included in Edward Marsh's 1910 volume *Georgian Poetry.* There is a constant loneliness, a perpetual exclusion of her from the ordinary ceremonies of life. She could be the uninvited guest in Michael Schmidt's eloquent and desolate lines from his poem "Choosing a Guest": *Absence I will invite. / I will invite / The morning birds, and I will not ask her.*

And then there is the issue of both gender and sexuality—neither overtly disclosed in the poems, but nevertheless the weather of many of them. Mew's sexuality is at once secretive and hiding in plain sight. It discloses itself, not as actions or partnerships, but as subtle obsessions of light and view; transgressions of feeling, as in "On the Road to the Sea" where she imagines the childhood of the person she fantasizes about. The ideas are not comfortable, but they are—as is so much in Mew—immediate and arresting.

I would have liked (so vile we are!) to have taught you tears.

III

Trying to pick up Mew's trail as a young woman is difficult. It would be almost impossible without some essays and introductions and information. Above all there is Penelope Fitzgerald's splendid and affectionate book *Charlotte Mew and Her Friends*, with its fine preface by Brad Leithauser. And, of course, Val Warner's essential, meticulous editing of *Collected Poems and Prose*. There is also the detailed and fascinating website kept at Middlesex University called "Charlotte's Web." Out of these accounts, a few details gleam.

Here, for instance, is Charlotte Mew asking Henry Harland, the editor of *The Yellow Book*, to pay her all at once for "Passed." Here she is falling in love with his secretary, Ella D'Arcy, who leaves London to live in the Channel Islands. There she is, just out of reach of her friends, rolling her own cigarettes, swearing forcefully, and dressing in darker and more masculine clothes by the day. And here she is again writing about Emily Brontë for the journal *Temple Bar* in 1904.

It is a short essay. But one sentence comes to life and turns its prophetic head. It looks back at the fragile, desolate young woman who wrote it: "Her nature stood alone," she writes of Brontë. "That was the awful fact—the tragedy of her life."

IV

We are now coming to that part of Mew's story which shows her at her most abandoned. Any account of her life at this point has to be grim. It has to be constructed with a bleak horizon, the way Anne Carson configures Emily Brontë's biographers in her powerful and wrenching poem "The Glass Essay":

This sad stunted life, says one.
Uninteresting, unremarkable, wracked by disappointment
and despair, says another.

Mew's was indeed a life of terrible loneliness. It was not simply that she was lesbian in a time of repression and restriction. There is also her social personality. She was a strange and volatile mix of attributes: she had a fierce, structured religious faith. It connected her to a visionary sense of order. It also dissociated her from the body. In the best of Mew's poetry these contradictions play off each other. There is an off-kilter fervor about her eroticism, and an erotic yearning to her spiritual world.

Nevertheless, in a plain and poignant sense, she found little peace or renewal within her sexuality. *Who would / have guessed / it possible / that waiting / is sustainable?* writes Kay Ryan in her compelling and moving poem "Patience." But for Mew patience is unrewarded. She made a series of approaches and received a series of rebuffs. She went from London to Paris in 1902 to join Ella D'Arcy, the former secretary to Henry Harland of *The Yellow Book.* She was excited, hopeful, tentative. But Ella D'Arcy was heterosexual and Mew shrank back. Years later, the same thing would happen in her relations with May Sinclair—an ardent affection would be turned away. In that case it was more public and still more humiliating. In fact, one of Sinclair's friends noted with asperity in her diary, "Charlotte is a pervert." In Mew's own poignant phrase she had "made herself damn ridiculous."

It was obvious she was looking for freedom and experiment, as well as an intellectual acceptance of her own sexuality. But in that closed era it eluded her. We have to imagine the rented rooms and seaside hotels and friends' houses in which she received the rejections which terrified her. But if she lost her sense of sexual dignity there, she also found, in that ordeal, one of her most convincing poems.

I remember rooms that have had their part
In the steady slowing down of the heart.
The room in Paris, the room at Geneva,
The little damp room with the seaweed smell,
And that ceaseless maddening sound of the tide
Rooms where for good or ill things died.

V

In 1915 Mew was invited to the Poetry Bookshop on the Strand, owned by Alida Monro's husband. Through the door came a tiny, strange woman, not more than four foot ten inches. "Her face was a fine oval," writes Monro, "and she always wore a little, hard pork-pie hat put on very straight." On that first occasion, Monro asked her if she was Charlotte Mew. She replied with a smile, saying "I am sorry to say I am."

Mew was nearly fifty when her first book *The Farmer's Bride* was published by Harold Monro's press. The year was 1916. It came out as a chapbook, in a coarse, gunmetal-colored jacket. The cover shows a child's drawing of a house. The roof slopes towards two small windows. A pair of fork-sharp trees are behind it. Next to the logo of "The Poetry Book Shop" is the inky symbol of a shilling.

It remains one of the most remarkable poetry publications

of the first half of the twentieth century. The edition of 1916 contains just seventeen poems. Some of them—"In Nunhead Cemetery," "The Farmer's Bride," "Madeleine in Church"— are signature Mew poems. Others are shorter. Most have her bleak strength. In 1921 the volume was re-issued with eleven new poems, keeping its name in the UK, but titled *Saturday Market* in the U.S. Much later, *The Collected Poems* was published in both countries, but not until 1953.

There are two stories folded into Mew's astonishing book, one visible and the other hidden. The first is of a compelling, lapsed lyric poet, a writer of harsh lines and scalding images who sought out—unusually in a time of Georgian sentiment—Hardy's darkness and offered herself as its inheritrix. Mew wrote an odd line—long and wayward, and far more voice-driven than was common in that era:

Do you remember the two old people we passed on the road to Kerity
Resting their sack on the stones, by the drenched wayside?

In the spirit of Hardy, her best poems show her ability to write a lurid pastoral—not the quiet celebration of England from a Victorian instruction set, but poems furnished with madhouses, broken spirits, unrecoverable partings. And yet her poems can also have an ominous pre-Audenesque elegance of tone.

It has been quiet as the country-side
Since Ted and Janey and then Mother died
And Tom crossed Father and was sent away.

But it is together, rather than singly, that the poems in this book open out into the second story—the one which is less visible, the one which helps to make Mew such an essential figure.

VI

The nineteenth century was a time of sinister enchantment for women poets. As if by sorcery, they ceased to be poets and became "poetesses." One by one, Christina Rossetti, Elizabeth Barrett Browning, and even Emily Brontë (at least in her poems) surrendered to a limiting sub-category: one designed by an anxious empire to reconcile acts of imagination with the obedience normally required of daughters and wives. During their courtship, Elizabeth Barrett, as she still was, wrote to Robert Browning:

> Thus you have an immense grasp in Art; and no one at all accustomed to consider the usual forms of it could help regarding with reverence and gladness the gradual expansion of your powers. Then you are "masculine" to the height—and I, as a woman, have studied some of your gestures of language and intonation wistfully, as a thing beyond me far! and the more admirable for being beyond.

A sinister enchantment? When Elizabeth Barrett wrote in one of her first letters to Robert Browning that her spirits drooped to the ground "like an untrained honeysuckle," she offered the quintessential image of the poetess. But it was more than a social expectation. The subtle, continuous, offset and interplay all through the nineteenth century of expectations of the poetess led directly to the lyric of pious love, and

sacred surrender: the four-stress, eight-beat line of an obedient music.

Then the break came. But how? By any logic, only a
woman poet so estranged from the society which constructed
the category could begin to dismantle its expectations. Charlotte Mew fits that description. Ironically she possessed, in
all her powerlessness, the requisite power: she could prove
the category deficient. And she did. The great unshackling of
women's voices in poetry has one of its beginnings right here.
These beautiful poems are full of rendings and breakings and
burnings.

Charlotte Mew lived for twelve more years after *The
Farmer's Bride*. In the spring of 1928, after the death of her
sister, she entered a nursing home in Beaumont Street. She
stayed there, in a shuttered room for weeks. In March, at the
threshold of spring, she left the house on a Saturday morning
to make a purchase. She bought a bottle of Lysol—a creosote mixture—and drank a small glass of it. She died, foaming
from the mouth, a few hours later. There is no bleaker death
in the history of poetry.

Mew built her poems in a radical and prescient way. She
had little imaginative loyalty to narrative traditions or lyric
inheritance. She was a maverick with rhetorical strategies.
A poem like "On the Road to the Sea"—which is typical of
her longer work—begins with a suppressed narrative, moves
quickly to a lyric sketch of childhood and back to a darker
mix of both. Then the tone can change again. She can sound
as surreal, as whimsical as Medbh McGuckian. But she is not
an imagist in the way that Medbh McGuckian is, who stores
an elaborate series of meanings into her comment on a dead
butterfly:

Its silence like the green cocoon of the car-wash,
Its passion for water to uncloud.

Mew stored her meanings in voice rather than image. She talked down her fears, and ratcheted up her rhetoric. She broke apart trains of thought and threw away structured linework. In this way, a portrait of erotic obsession is rescued from a conventional framework. Mew is not a modernist. But she has an acute sense of how to set up an alliance with fragmentation.

There is a sort of salt and spray about reading Mew for the first time: her poems are not like anything else. No reading of Victorian or Edwardian poetry prepares for them. If the big, wilful lines, the direct voice seem like transgressions, it is because they are. They have enough force to unwrite the false pastorals of Georgian England and the dead sweetness of pre-modernist, post-Victorian poetry.

I found Mew's work in my thirties—a poem here and there. Its effect was gradual, not sudden. I wished then, as I do now, that I had found it in some compact and available form when I was a beginning poet. Its courage and plainspoken syntax would certainly have affected me.

But I didn't read those poems at a formative moment. I hope that new readers will. I can imagine the effect. Fortunately, I don't need to find words for it. The description of how these poems might reach their audience is already there in Mew's essay on Brontë. "When first we read these songs," she writes, all the way back in 1904, "we are brought face to face with the woman who wrote them. And when once we know them and have been haunted by their rebellious and contending music it will not be possible to forget."

The Other Sylvia Plath

In 1952 Randall Jarrell published an essay called "The Other Robert Frost." In it, he put before the reader the dark and layered vision—"the bare sorrow," as he called it—of Frost's best poems. It was Jarrell's way of trying to alter the perception that Frost was a facile, one-note lyricist. This essay is named for that one, in recognition of Jarrell's commitment to the deception and complication of a poet's achievement. And, even more so, in honor of Sylvia Plath's complex, radical poems of motherhood.

In the decade following the English publication of *Ariel*, a critical response to Plath's work began to form in articles and essays. Most of it shared the characteristics which still haunt her work; or at least its transmission. First, that her early critics refused to consider her poems apart from her suicide. And second, most of them glued the poems of *Ariel* to the poet-image of Plath in the last three months of her life. These small critical detours led to large errors in the critique of Plath's work.

The truth is that if the critical horizon had stretched back another twelve weeks, something else would have become visible. The image of a desperate woman in a London flat, exhausted by weather and hard-to-get child care, would have shimmered and dissolved into something else: into a poet and mother under the big stars of southwest England, in a beautiful October. A poet who, for all the shock and distress of her situation, was trying hopeful and daring things in language.

I am writing the best poems of my life, they will make my name, she wrote in a letter during this month. A poet who, together with the poems of public rhetoric and gesture she wrote during these weeks—such as "Lady Lazarus" and "Daddy"—was also testing out a new and powerful language in poems like "Nick and the Candlestick" and "Night Dances" and "By Candlelight." And who, in these private and path-breaking poems of motherhood, transformed the traditional nature poem—the location of its speaker and its inherited landscape. Unfortunately, the writer of these October nature poems is not as convenient to myth-making as the distraught and self-destructive sibyl. Even now, Plath's legend refuses to allow the second version to complete the first. But this is the poet I have loved and admired. This is the other Plath.

I was eighteen when Plath died. She was then twelve years older than me. I say *then* because time has moved on, my life has progressed within it, and yet she has remained a gifted, changeless, broken young woman of thirty.

The winter of 1962 quickly became notorious in Ireland and England. She died at the bitter end of it, literally—in those first few days of February when snowdrops are already out and when the first crocuses are beginning to show their purples and orange-yellows at the roadsides. The end came quickly. There was no time even to say, as Anne Sexton does in "Demon," *Oh demon within / I am afraid.*

It was a freakish season. I was in my first year of university in Dublin. By November a smoky frost was refusing to clear even by noon. At night the railings around Stephen's Green produced a tearing cold on the fingertips. But October was beautiful and unusual. The air was glittery and defined; it was clear and bitter. The rain held off. October was also the last month Plath spent at Court Green, the house in Devon she and Ted Hughes had bought the previous year. Her son had been born there. Her marriage had faltered there. Now she was packing, sheeting and closing it to go to London. In the small village of North Tawton, five hours from London and an hour from the Atlantic coast of England, she began the poems which would become *Ariel*.

In some ways the house was a liability—large, unheated and with no radiators. In the downstairs rooms, so her letters say, the temperature was thirty-eight degrees. The windows would have opened back into the fog of those orchards: into *a thick, gray death-soup*, as she called it in "Letter in November."

But in that beautiful October there must also have been small winter revelations. White fields in the morning. Windfalls glowing through fog. Huge stars at night. The first winter of her baby son Nick. She was already preparing a language for the season. *In a forest of frost, in a dawn of cornflowers*, she wrote at the end of "Poppies in October."

The extraordinary energies she tapped into in this month led her to write "By Candlelight" on October 24th, "Nick and the Candlestick" on the 28th, and just a few days into the next month, "Night Dances." Ten days at most separate these poems. They are as intense as any cluster of lyrics in

Ariel. They have a common vocabulary and a shared strength. In her BBC broadcast in the following month she spoke with unusual directness of her strategy and purpose. *A mother nurses her baby son by candlelight,* she said, *and finds in him a beauty which, while it may not ward off the world's ill, does redeem her share of it.*

As a reader, I often return there: to that creaking wintry house, to the estrangement of this young woman in a place which was not her own, looking for words which were. Here if anywhere it is appropriate to ask the question: What is it that changes when a woman poet becomes a mother? What is it that alters, shifts, turns the poem around? The answer must be—and Plath's poems are the model for it—that suddenly the nature poem opens to her. Suddenly this poem defined by history, withheld by custom, is hers. All hers.

The nature poem. So inscribed, so written, so set into the tradition of poetry that it can look like an arcane code. But it is not arcane. In fact, the nature poem is volatile: an accurate register of cultural and historic change. Before the Industrial Revolution it was a pastoral poem; and after it a pessimistic one. It has always been there, in the center of the action. Like other poetic conventions, it has its roots in deeply human things. Change those things, alter that angle, and the roots will shift, ready to be put somewhere else.

I believe Plath—the other Plath—changed the nature poem. She shifted its course. She re-directed its historic energy. *Ariel* may seem a slim text to argue with. Then again, many of the shape-changing texts of nature poetry—whether *The Lyrical Ballads* or *North of Boston*—are modest, apparently unimposing single volumes. Unimposing that is, until you read them.

No definition will put the tradition of the nature poem

neatly in context. It is baggy, vast, hard to collect in one place. In its sober discussion of it, the *Princeton Encyclopedia of Poetry and Poetics* registers the swerves and changes of nature poets as well as poems: *They strongly feared*—this about the Romantic poets—*that men merely read meaning into a deterministic and meaningless world.* Of Eliot and Crane: *The typical nature of 20th century poetry is that of T. S. Eliot's* The Waste Land *and Hart Crane's* The Bridge, *where the natural—and human—world is conceived of as shattered, fragmentary, painful.*

These words offer a clue, if not a proof. Traditionally most nature poems share a common feature: they are written by poets willing to be instructed by nature—whether in dark apprehension, like Frost, or towards an ethical direction like Wordsworth. Some of the best twentieth-century nature poems—Lowell's "Skunk Hour" for instance—are an account, not so much of nature, but of that instruction set.

Plath changed this. As the moon rises over a baby boy in "Nick and the Candlestick," as the stars plummet, as a blue light wanders to the window and then retreats, the landscape shifts and changes. By the time we turn back from the charm and power of the poem, something else has changed as well: the instruction set. This is no longer a poet being instructed by nature. This is a poet instructing nature. How did this happen? Plath was a shrewd and obdurate crafter of poems. But she was not theoretical and her aesthetic sense was instinctive. How did she come upon this radical, swift strategy that made these beautiful, shape-changing diagrams of the nature poem? *How?*

Years ago I interviewed John Ashbery for the *Irish Times*. He was reading in a small market town to the south of Dublin. It took me about an hour to drive down. It was a drizzling, shimmering spring afternoon. Many of his answers about his work and his aesthetic were eloquent. One in particular stuck with me for years. I asked him whether he was a surrealist and he told me that he himself had asked the French poet Henri Michaux the same question. No, Michaux replied, he was not a surrealist. But, for him, surrealism had been *la grande permission*.

La grande permission. I believe this is exactly what Plath found in these poems which kept crowding into her last October. Her motherhood gave her a sense of her own nature. Her nature in turn gave her a sense of participation in the power and mystery of seasons and arrivals. Plath's strategy, as I see it, has rippled out; it has made an influential change.

I see it again in the way Louise Glück fills a poem like "All Hallows" with a voice that controls the natural world, rather than being controlled by it: *Even now this landscape is assembling. / The hills darken. / The oxen sleep in their blue yoke.* Or, to shift a tone and theme, the way Brenda Hillman writes with a bright authority in her poem "Mighty Forms": *However we remember California later / the earth we loved will know the truth: / that it wanted us back for itself.* Women now seem to write the nature poem from a different angle. It is hard not to believe that in those cold rooms in Devon, alone as she was, Plath began that intensely sociable change. No longer, in her version of the nature poem, is the poet instructed by nature. In the few lines, the few poems of that month, the speaker *is* nature.

Plath wrote "By Candlelight" on October 24, 1962, the day before her birthday. The next day she would be thirty. It is the least compelling of the three poems. Some of the cartoonish language of her early work is still in evidence. The internal rhymes are crude, the cadences are choppy, but there is an exhilarating freedom as well: if this is a cartoon, then it points the way towards bigger, more somber work.

The scene is a nursery room at night—full of shadows

and bells, with a candlestick near the cot. *The candlestick was a small brass image of Hercules*, wrote Ted Hughes in the notes to the *Collected Poems—in his lion's pelt, kneeling under the candle. Behind his heels five brass balls completed the design.*

If the language is occasionally uncertain, the stance of Plath as nature poet is anything but. This is a speaker with a new kind of control: able to command the natural world because she herself is generative of it. As a mother with her child—at the very center of that world—she can speak about seasons and times with a new freedom and invention. She can fit in fabrics and tapestries, the dark outside and the light inside. Despite the hardship and cold of these days, her zest for the world evokes the eloquence of Lucille Clifton's lines from "cutting greens": *and i taste in my natural appetite / the bond of live things everywhere.*

Here truly is a female Prospero, speaking from her shipwrecked island, never doubting that the elements will obey her. Where other nature poets have labored for imitation or even awe, she will have none of it. This nature poem is an act of power, not deference. But the power is not simply in the aesthetic. It is in the sounds also, with their deft mixing of conversation and cadence, proving just how reliable is Seamus Heaney's assertion that Plath was "a poet governed by the auditory imagination."

> *This is winter, this is night, small love—*
> *A sort of black horsehair,*
> *A rough, dumb country stuff*

If I could, I would re-construct those last days of October 1962 in Devon. In photographs, Court Green, under its giant wych elm, shows off its thatched roof, its unsparing stone exterior. Now, as the month drew on, the cold rooms would have seemed harbingers of winter. Plath had cleaned and painted them the previous year. Now she must have stood in them, looking out the windows. Seeing a landscape through her language. In England, at that time of year, low cloud would have covered the fields long past dawn. But equally, when dark came, the skies must have been laundered by early frosts. Here at the start of winter, in the upstairs room where her baby son slept, where she revised her poems, the acoustics must have been made of the sound of freezing air and the squeak of starlight.

Sometime on the 29th of October, Plath finished revising "Nick and the Candlestick." It assembles the most disparate lyric elements imaginable: with a few bold strokes of language and music, a dark room and a sleeping baby are made over into a cave and its treasure. A big narrative unfolds, and a breathtakingly odd one.

I am a miner. The light burns blue.
Waxy stalactites
Drip and thicken

Plath's statement in a BBC interview done on October 30, just a day after completing the poem, bears repeating here: *In this poem a mother nurses her baby son by candlelight and finds in him a beauty which, while it may not ward off the world's ill, does redeem her share of it.*

Let the stars plummet
To their dark address

Let the mercuric
Atoms that cripple drip
Into the terrible well

You are the one
Solid the spaces lean on, envious.

So many conventions of the nineteenth-century nature poem give, yield, slide away here. As if Plath had put her hand to a secret door, an entrance into a possibility that had remained hidden in poetry; shut fast until this moment. Do I think Plath's motherhood brought her there? Of course. But nothing is as single or simple as that in poetry. There were other powerful agents in the shifting of voice and location: for instance, Plath may not have been a surrealist in the strict meaning of the term. She might not even have responded to Michaux's term of *la grande permission*. But for all that, these poems show the signature intelligence of the committed surrealist: a sensibility hostile to the official measurements and surfaces of the world; a freedom in re-arranging those surfaces; a determination to make the natural world dream with her. These are so evident in the third poem from this group, "The Night Dances," that it becomes impossible to ignore the powerful convergence between motherhood and modes of surrealism in Plath's final work:

"The Night Dances" has a plain enough starting point. A baby boy gets up in his cot, swivels and gestures and turns as if he was dancing. *A revolving dance which her baby son performed at night in his crib*, writes Hughes in his note. But plain or not, this is Plath's great poem of motherhood. This is where all nature is summoned, invoked, sent away and then recalled. At first it seems the dances are geometry rather than anything else:

And how will your night dances
lose themselves? In mathematics?

After this initial meditation, Plath opens out the poem into an astonishing fission of suggestions, associations, fragments and dream parts. The fragrance of the sleeping child is like lilies—but no, because lilies fold into coldness and egotism, and then the tiger's spots are violences, but also refer again to the flowers.

Then all at once, the earth leans back and looks up. The infant's gestures become planetary signs—figuring back into a mysterious space, where perhaps they came from. But once there, the spinning stops: geometry and nature are re-united.

> *Why am I given*
> *These lamps, these planets*
> *Falling like blessings, like flakes*

Plath lived and died in a world that thought about poets in one way, although her poems pointed in another direction. Her posthumous reputation has suffered from a romantic expectation which her cooler, more rigorous adventures as a poet had no opportunity to change. Years have passed. The stars of southwest England still look down. The house in Devon is still there. But now both its poet-owners are dead. At last a wider and more enquiring look at Plath's work can show that those months she spent there in October 1962—as young poet and high-wire surrealist—produced poems which open out the whole question of how a new possession of nature has made a new nature poem. This is a radical change. In this way, poetry is like progress: it can never turn back.

It stands to reason: That a young poet-mother, in an English pre-winter, with her baby boy and the clear-skied darks had enough leverage to shift an ancient convention, should not be a surprise. This is the way change in poetry always occurs. The only surprise should be how little was made of it at the time. But the poems are there: the skies are dark and frost still descends over that part of Devon. The little boy still swerves and turns in his cot. That marvelous young woman lives and speaks every time one of these poems is read. The words are changeless. It is only poetry that has been changed.

The Case of
Edna St. Vincent Millay

I

This is a strange story. If it were set in a Victorian gaslight novel it might have dark corners and a gloomy conclusion. In an equivalent from the American 1930s it would have a missing woman and tough-talking detectives. But genre fiction is not the purpose of this piece. This is the story of a poet who achieved extraordinary fame and glamour in her twenties. Who held the imagination of her time in a solid poise between respect and fascination. This is a story of contradictions and illusions. Of a poet who commanded a popular following at the wrong moment. Of a contemporary writer with a modern sensibility whose diction remained arcane.

What happened to Millay has come to interest me because she seemed to disappear. After the beacon brightness of her presence in the first decades of this century she fell from conversation and curricula. Most of all, she fell from serious discussion. Whenever I look at the work of women poets—sifting, revisiting—hers seems to me the most poignant and contradictory. I believe that in her work—and its transmission—a confluence of permissions and their lack, tolerance and its lack, canonical power and its abuse come together.

This piece, therefore, is an attempt to puzzle out her meaning. As an Irish poet, reading her work from a distance, I am sure I missed some signals. And yet I am equally sure Millay can be read across borders. My interests in this piece are precisely that: to cross borders of time and location in an attempt to find her poems and her witness. To use her as a compass to chart a path through an immediate poetic past. I believe that a closer look at Millay opens up a different view of what happened in contemporary poetry. But where to begin?

Camden. Perched above Penobscot bay in Maine. This is one beginning. A road goes up the slope of a hill road to the Whitehall Inn. It was a resort hotel at the turn of the twentieth century. A few years ago I went there with a friend. I wanted to see the bay and the islands. Above all I wanted to be in the room in the inn where Millay's future was arranged one summer evening in 1912, when she was nineteen years of age.

The hotel, when I got there, had just opened for the summer. The man behind the counter had a breezy, start-of-season friendliness. He stood in a circular reception area. I asked about Millay and explained my interest. He bent down, rummaged for a minute and then straightened and handed me a folder. Its cover was red plastic, stretched to bursting around its contents which were ineffectively bound by ribbon. Inside were letters and photographs and newspaper cuttings.

I took the folder to the window and put it on a table. It was a strange moment. I had come to this part of Maine in a cold early summer. I had wanted to see the town, and this place most of all—this little hotel up a steep incline. I had come looking for evidence of a poet whose chances and choices had crossed here on a summer night. What I found was something different. Here, on the table, was a debris of signatures, newsprint, photographs, letters. There was nothing dignified or even literary about it. This could have been the attic collection of a neglected aunt—a shoebox's worth of a life.

I put the folder around its papers, handed it to the man and walked to the photographs on the wall. They were hung in neat, plain frames. One showed Millay standing with other high school students on the front grass. It was hard to fit this vivid long-ago New England girl with the randomness of the papers, the lack of ceremony. But that's what I had come to do: to try to associate and explain—at least to myself. Over a few years, my interest in Millay had become sharper, more focused. For me—although I was born in Ireland and responsive to a different literary tradition—she constituted a vital piece of missing information.

Edna St. Vincent Millay came to Camden in childhood. Her father, Henry Millay, was a teacher and school superintendent, her mother a nurse. When she was eight her father left the family. Later she remembered his actual departure "across a swamp of cranberries." On the May afternoon I was there you could look down from Mount Battie to something very near to what Millay herself must have seen: the up-and-down masts of yachts bobbing in the harbor. And farther out the blue shapes of islands.

She went to the local high school there and watched her sisters while her mother worked at night as a nurse. It was Millay's mother who in 1911 prepared the first change in her daughter's life. She pointed her towards a poetry contest which would result in her inclusion in a book. The book was to be called *The Lyric Year*. It was to contain the hundred best poems published in the United States in the previous twelve months. Submissions were invited by the publisher, Mitchell Kennerley. Millay sent in the poem she had just finished, called "Renascence." Although she did not win, her poem was accepted for inclusion in the book.

The town of Camden had been a shipping and whaling center through much of the nineteenth century. Six-masted schooners were built there and launched on their journeys to India and China. Towards the end of the century, Camden took on another Cinderella-like identity. During the summer, as if the pages of a Wharton novel had opened and allowed its characters to wander northwards, a stream of New York visitors arrived to take the sea air.

On the night of August 29, 1912, each of the girls who had worked in the hotel for the summer had to perform an end-of-season piece: a song or a recitation. Norma Millay had worked there all summer. And now she persuaded her sister to be one of the performers as well. Edna came and sat at the revolving piano stool and spun around on it and recited "Renascence."

The poem had already been published in *The Lyric Year*. But this was a different form of publication: a room full of smoke and laughter and money. A girl of nineteen putting her view of the local into a visual language for the transients. A girl who had never been far from this seascape scoring its claustrophobia and charm as the clean, surprising octosyllabic paragraph of the opening.

All I could see from where I stood
Was three long mountains and a wood.

I turned and looked another way
And saw three islands in a bay.

As a result of the recitation a woman came forward at the end of the evening to speak to Millay. Her name was Caroline Dow, head of the National Training School of the Young Women's Christian Association in New York. She spoke to Millay, urged her to go to college and promised she would do her best to assist her financially. In that room, at that moment, Millay's life swerved.

1912 was a turning point in more than Millay's life. With two years to go to the Great War, the air was full of change and omen. The *Titanic* sank. Home Rule was passed for Ireland. The Olympic Games took place in Stockholm. But underneath these public events ran another volatile stream of expressive upheaval. It had been in the air since the new century. "Suddenly in 1900," wrote Yeats, "everybody got down from their stilts. Nobody drank absinthe anymore with his black coffee."

Now, in 1912, the pace quickened again. Poets emerged from their lairs and changed their habitats: Eliot left America and went to Paris and then to London. Robert Frost sold his farm in Derry, New Hampshire, and also sailed to England. Pound was only a year away from spending the winter with Yeats in Stone Cottage on the edge of Ashdown Forest. Back in Chicago, Harriet Monroe had returned from a trip to China and decided to begin a magazine of contemporary poetry. She sent out a circular promising poets "a chance to be heard in their own place."

In the Whitehall Inn, reciting her version of the local in the cadences of the familiar, Edna St. Vincent Millay knew little about these poetic changes. But personal change was happening. Caroline Dow's audience at that occasion, her random encounter with Millay, opened doors which would take Millay out of the small town.

It was a moment. And it was more than that. It was a collision of freedoms happening in an atmosphere—characteristic of Millay's early life—of chance and drama. Because of her recitation, because of the presence of Caroline Dow there that night, Millay would go to Vassar. She would receive an education.

But ironically, as those freedoms were opening up for her, the changes in the poetry world—all of them still invisible to a nineteen-year-old—were ensuring that other opportunities were shutting down. Out beyond that room, with its merriment and conversation, poetry was beginning one of its most turbulent historic passages. The poem would change; the audience would change. Millay could not have known that summer night that as her personal world opened up, her poetic one was becoming a prison.

Millay was twenty-one when she went to Vassar. Her college career was turbulent and her letters reflect her ambivalence. "I hate this pink-and-gray college," she wrote in her first year. She graduated in 1917 and almost at once published her first book, *Renascence*, to acclaim. For a brief moment, contrary forces came together to praise it. Some contemporary critics like Louis Untermeyer complained about a straining after effect. But Millay's poems had already begun their rare passage in the world: already they were moving through the permeable membrane between poem and audience; already they had become part of the process which transports words out of a book and into the speech and memory of everyday life.

"Here is a very exceptional first book, a book which is achievement rather than promise," wrote Harriet Monroe.

"One would have to back a long way in literary history to find a young poet singing so freely and musically in such a big world." And certainly, in many of the shorter poems in *Renascence* it's possible to see the charms and problems of Millay's work already on show. The superb, conversational music. The quick-witted turn in a narrow stanza. The fast-shunt rhyme and clever, close-quarters rhetoric. Already Millay could write an uncluttered, ringing line in a memorable way. Characteristically, she did much better with the beat and stutter of a short line than with a long one. By the end of the year her first book was finding its path. And she was trying to do the same.

Millay moved to Greenwich Village in the winter of 1917. Almost at once she became part of a rare congruence in American culture. The irregular tangle of streets south of West Fourteenth Street had once provided residences for wealthy New Yorkers. By the turn of the century they were long gone and the Village was a maze of unheated apartments, theaters and cafes.

Millay was a vocal, visible presence. She first lived at Waverly Place in a single room. Later she moved to West Twelfth Street, decorated her apartment in Chinese style and entertained her admirers. Edmund Wilson puts her further away. "She was hard up," he writes, "and lived with her mother and sisters at the very end of West Nineteenth Street." The actual location hardly matters. What mattered was that she was writing herself into the American moment.

One cold, northerly spring a sculptor came to Dublin. I was in my early twenties. The sculptor, an American woman, was anxious to model younger Irish writers for a series of heads she was doing. I agreed to sit for her. It didn't even seem a strange request. My mother had been a painter. My childhood was full of failed attempts to sit still.

I went for a few hours on separate mornings to the sculptor's hotel. She worked quickly. Our conversation was anecdotal. But one morning, almost by chance, she told me that a poet—later a celebrated woman poet—had recited her poetry in her mother's drawing room in New York. Almost her first poetry reading, she said. The poet—she added these details—wore flowing clothes and had a deep voice. She was a thrilling reader. She was young then, she added; very young. Her name was Edna St. Vincent Millay.

I was disconcerted. In some irrational way, I was also disappointed. I hardly ever heard accounts of women poets. I was hungry for news of this rare species, to which by now I was sure I belonged. There were not many women poets in Ireland. I had no news of them elsewhere either. Now here was one, fixed by anecdote, and somehow unappealing.

My reaction was a mix of superstition and memory. I was the daughter of a diplomat. I had put behind me my childhood with its endlessly arriving visitors. I had recently graduated from Trinity. I knew Yeats by heart and was about to be married. Here in the small, charged city of Dublin where the life of the writer seemed a self-conscious pageant, I was trying to fit in. Why on earth, I thought, would a poet want to go back to a drawing room, to wearing long dresses and declaiming her poetry?

Now, of course, so many years later, the sculptor's story leads to a series of connected rooms. It no longer seems to be about a woman and her patron. On the contrary it looks to be a snapshot of a habitat. Millay lived in Greenwich Village; she read her poems further uptown. She navigated simultaneous worlds with grace. And of necessity. Reading *Restless Spirit*, the biography of Millay by Miriam Gurko, I was able to connect the pieces. Speaking of Millay's first winter in New York in 1917, when she found it hard to get theatrical work, Gurko writes: "She kept going financially by giving readings of her poems."

A woman in long clothes. A poet in society drawing rooms. Millay is not a clear image at this stage of her life. This is not helped by the fact that the language her contemporaries use to describe her is both effusive and reductive. "The more I saw of this young and beautiful girl," writes Llewellyn Powys, "the more I came to appreciate the rash quality of her nature, heedless and lovely as the fieldfare rising out of the wintry ground." She had a lovely and very long throat that gave her the look of a muse," wrote Edmund Wilson. It is all unclear, to say the least.

But none of these comments obscures her as much as the theatricality of her diction. Millay had perfect pitch. Her lines are fast and musical. Her diction is another matter. The way a poet sites themselves in an angle towards contemporary speech matters. It becomes a register of its own response: of adventure, caution, response, failure of response. It gets inside a secret portion of art and purpose where the codes of language and desire are set.

Millay's diction is a puzzle. Her rhythmic sense pointed confidently towards a new age. Her diction reached back to an invented past. It is a confusing and unsettling part of her work. It may also have been a symptom rather than a cause. In a fine essay on Millay, Sandra Gilbert writes about the strains and expectations of the woman artist trapped "behind the rigid mask of a self that she flaunted but despised as inauthentic." Even at the end of a celebrated sonnet, beginning "What lips my lips have kissed," Millay selects an unsettling elevation of tone:

I cannot say what loves have come and gone,
I only know that summer sang in me
A little while, that in me sings no more.

In 1920 Millay published a small volume of poems with a vivid green cover. The print run was a thousand copies. It sold out almost at once. Like her previous books it came out with Mitchell Kennerley. Two years later Harper & Brothers would acquire her copyright. But in 1920 *A Few Figs from Thistles* crept into the world, still a chapbook, almost a throwaway gesture.

Like the rest of Millay's work, it was uneven. But the successful poems had a new and darker wit. They were startling and memorable. For the first time in a decade, the absence of any need to strike a romantic pose liberated her into a compelling tone shift. Suddenly Millay stumbles into an historic center of poetry: a place where the public life of an age ends and the popular lyric begins. Where the poet enters an intense musical partnership with a community of readers. Here at last is a place where, to paraphrase Christian Wiman in his fine poem "From a Window," an audience can be transformed into *countless beings of one mind*. So much so that a lyric may even be said to be co-authored by that partnership. From the troubadours to the Irish balladeers of 1798, so many poems constitute the lost cities of that lyric. Now in this book, Millay stands on the same ground; an inspired archaeologist.

My candle burns at both ends.
It will not last the night.
But ah my foes and oh my friends
It gives a lovely light.

This seam of lyric exuberance continues through the book. "A Portrait by a Neighbor," for instance, creates a magical, off-kilter snapshot of Millay herself:

> *She digs in her garden*
> *With a shovel and spoon*
> *She weeds her lazy lettuce*
> *By the light of the moon.*

The lighthearted tone and confrontational rhetoric, put together with Millay's perfect ear, destabilizes poetic conventions, including myth. Her poem "Daphne" is a model of elegance and compression:

> *Yet if over hill and hollow*
> *Still it is your will to follow,*
> *I am off;—to heel Apollo!*

The poems in *A Few Figs from Thistles* burn off the mists surrounding Millay's first poetic persona. The outline is sharp and clear. The voice is audible, freed from the muffle and clutter of her previous diction. At the center of the book is the wonderful, do-or-die "Recuerdo," with its good-natured hexameters and surreal images of New York.

> *We were very tired, we were very merry—*
> *We had gone back and forth all night on the ferry.*
> *It was bare and bright, and smelled like a stable—*
> *But we looked into a fire, we leaned across a table,*
> *We lay on a hill-top underneath the moon;*
> *And the whistles kept blowing, and the dawn came soon.*

II

Why write about Millay? She is uneven. Her later work is unconvincing. Her reputation is problematic. But I have been drawn to her from the start partly because of her vivid spirit, partly because of a compelling and indispensable handful of poems. But also, because she is—in poetic terms—the scene of the crime.

When I was a young poet, I spent more time than I wanted trying to find my way in an intensely political and national poetic culture. The form I saw around me—the poem of the day—was so often taken over by public feelings and cultural prescription that I was unsure where the poetic energies of that lyric began and the public life of its ethos ended.

At the end of a day, in a city whose literary culture became increasingly exasperating to me, it was not unusual for someone to turn aside from a conversation in a pub or in the blue air of a smoky room and suddenly recite verses while others nodded and supplied lines and interjected comments. If I had only known it then, Ireland was one of the last places where there was a shelter for the lyric poem in its public and cultural guise. I was, whether I knew it or not, in a throwback culture.

Little by little, the dominant culture came calling. All that had happened in twentieth-century poetry would prevail over my first encounters with Irish poetry, and make me look more squarely at the world the Irish enclave was hidden from. Gradually I would see the powerful and expansionist claims of twentieth-century modernism.

And this is where Millay comes in: she is a case study I

could never have observed in Ireland. She suggests an alternative narrative for what happened in poetry in this century. Millay became subject to choices and critiques which no poet in the English-speaking world would afterwards be able to ignore.

Modernism had two great projects. If this seems like a broad statement, I have no feeling I should apologize for it. After all, as a working poet, I lived in the light of the first and the shadow of the second. It left me free to be a witness to both.

The first project could not be contested. It was to re-make the poem so that it could speak to the world it originated in; so that it could converse more honestly with its own past. This purpose involved poets like Pound, Eliot and Yeats—and later others—in a struggle of will and conscience and courage.

If this was all, poetry would now be a coherent entity. The scalding and beautiful poems of the modernist poets changed an entire art. They demonstrated a new inclusiveness; they promised a bolder and less reverent relation to history. They broke ground. They showed the way.

Modernism's second project, however, seems less clear and conscientious. This is the one I felt as a shadow; this is the one that shadowed Millay. Its purpose was to re-make, not the poem, but the reader of the poem. This—as the arguments of modernist critics began to make clear—meant detaching the reader from the old popular expectations of the poem.

What did this mean? What effect did it have? To start with, it required a readership to forget a vast, sun-splashed hinterland. A place where the poet and balladeer shaped the day's events. It meant forgetting the front rooms where poems were once recited at the end of festivities. Where couplets were summoned to memory at a christening or a wedding. Where quatrains were tossed half-spoken into a group of people who completed them. It meant, above all, cutting the reader away from the historic connection between poet and audience. It meant laying aside the old and hallowed relation between the reader and the memory of a poem, which had been for hundreds of years one of the true archives of poetry.

This second project was not visible when *A Few Figs from Thistles* was published. It came later. Even then it showed up merely in wish lists. "We can only say that it appears likely that poets in our civilization, as it exists at present, must be *difficult*," wrote Eliot. "The poet must become more and more comprehensive, more allusive, more indirect, in order to force, to dislocate if necessary, language into his meaning."

Modernism's resistance to the popular audience had roots in a volatile past. David Perkins's comment in *A History of Modern Poetry* gives an interpretation of the developing rift. "There is some truth in the argument," he writes, "that high Modernist art was not simply unpopular, as any new art may be for a while, but antipopular."

Where did this leave Millay? In *A Few Figs from Thistles* she was the popular poet par excellence. Her vivid, racy cadences caught a popular mood. But the book also gestures more subtly towards the history of poetry. In all ages, at all times, the poet and the community have come together to be authors of certain poems. Have shared the task, the record and the memory. In this paradigm—as old as poetry itself—the job is divided: the poet finds the language, the community records it in memory.

Modernism resisted co-authorship. In essays by Allen Tate and Eliot, there is a persistent anxiety that the popular reader might hold back the progress of the emerging modernist poem. The mistake lay in the refusal to look both ways. To stare Janus-faced at the popular past as well as the challenging present. There was no need for one to disown the other. In calling this book *A Journey with Two Maps* I have attempted to show that one map of poetry is no longer enough. Another tradition, another possibility, a different direction keeps suggesting itself. Modernism did not consider it. And certain poets—Millay is one of them—suffered for that.

"Does anyone still discuss the work of Edna St. Vincent Millay as a serious contribution to modern poetry?" wrote Harold Orel in an essay on her. The critic Suzanne Clark notes, "Much after my first encounter with Millay, when I was in graduate school, I imagined I might study her verse. 'No,' advised my critical friends, 'Edna St. Vincent Millay is simply not interesting.'"

David Perkins, after a brief discussion of Millay in *A History of Modern Poetry*, locates what happened to her: "When Miss Millay's reputation began to decline the reason usually assigned by reviewers for rejecting where they had once praised was either that she had changed for the worse or, at least, had made no progress toward the better . . . In general, the evolution of her own poetry affected her reputation much less than the evolution of poetry at large. She lost ground because of the gradual acceptance in the late 1920s and 1930s of what I have called 'the high Modernist mode.'"

And yet Millay's work is compelling; it writes itself into memory. It allows and encourages questions. Readers and writers of poetry can start with them as soon as they put down *A Few Figs from Thistles*. They might ask, for instance: How do we want to map the future of poetry? How do we want to embark on another century's journey?

For myself I am clear: like many readers, I return to Millay—to her music, her courage, her witness. Her best work widens the sense, not just of what poetry says, but of what it is. More importantly, it suggests that whatever map we used which brought us to a point where a poet like Millay is becoming harder to locate needs to be re-drawn.

Denise Levertov:
Letters to a Broken World

I

Poetry and letter writing go together. The wit, candor and dailiness of poets' letters make them a necessary part of poetic history. They give us a homely view, recording Keats's wish to sit down to write in a clean shirt. Or Larkin's belief that he was constructing "a verbal device or machine." And yet for some reason there are fewer letter writers among women poets. In the twentieth century, those who belonged to this group, and whose letters have been made public, can be counted on one hand. Marianne Moore, Sylvia Plath, Elizabeth Bishop, Muriel Rukeyser—all these wrote letters of great interest. But it is a small number.

And they are not all the same. While Bishop and Plath chart a personal journey in their correspondence, the letters of Denise Levertov to Robert Duncan are different in kind. They flew back and forth in the fifties, sixties and seventies.

From Paris to New York. From London to Paris. From New York to Stinson Beach. They registered daily events: travel and empty wallets and weddings and new poems. They were of their time and bound by it. They belonged, among other things, to a vanishing social circumstance. They make up, as Adrienne Rich said, "a poetic legacy that exists partly thanks to a U.S. Postal Service that was at the time the cheapest, fastest communications game in the country."

But the importance of Levertov's letters are not in their frequency. The importance lies in their content. They track a quarrel which festered in twentieth-century poetry. And, because of that, festered between these poets. Duncan and Levertov lost a friendship because they could not agree on the poet's responsibility. But it was more than that. Their friendship dissolved because they could not consider the possibility that oppositional views, if looked at together, could enrich their understanding of the art they shared.

When *The Letters of Robert Duncan and Denise Levertov*, superbly edited by Robert J. Bertholf and Albert Gelpi, were published in 2003, they provided a unique glimpse into the drama and hurt they explored. The issue was clear. Two poets, Denise Levertov and Robert Duncan, began as friends and comrades in the business of poetry. They sustained each other with a unique generosity. But their long friendship ended in bitterness. As Michael Davidson said in his review of the book, "At the heart of their disagreement was the status of the poem, the extent to which poetry could be the vehicle for political views."

Levertov was a mercurial letter writer. Because I had known her slightly I could hear her voice in her letters. Reading the book made me remember a tone. It recalled a cold, sunshiny morning when I first met her. She had come over to Dublin to give a reading. It was the mid-1980s. I was there to interview her for the *Irish Times*. I drove to a house in Rathmines: a narrow cottage that seemed to have crouched down and missed the city-wreckers and building speculators. I found her in the front room, a smiling, debonair woman. She was quick of speech and witty. And she had an elusive air. What was it? At the time I was puzzled. Now I think, with her English birth, her American citizenship, her Russian inheritance, she was like one of those European exiles at a cafe table on a summer evening—able to understand every place because she had lost the ability to belong to only one.

The expatriate friendliness, the ease in several worlds was characteristic of Denise Levertov. But it concealed something else: a fierce sense of poetic tribe. An outsider's need to have a community of aesthetics. If she had lost a sense of country, she could still have one of cabal. That morning in Dublin she spoke of the Black Mountain School of Poetry. She mentioned her involvement with it in the fifties and sixties. I knew of it only in a distant way. I had come across it in journals and books. I thought of it as a radical initiative, a series of disruptive revisions of poetic practice.

And yet, that morning at least, there was nothing historical in the way she spoke. On the contrary, a strange tone of wistfulness crept into her conversation when she talked about a fellowship of craft and family feeling. She spoke of the inevitable divisions and strains of a poetic group. She mentioned a poet, Robert Duncan, whose name I knew slightly. But she paused on that name. He had been important to her, she said. They had quarreled. And he was ill at that moment. Even today, I remember the pause, the wistfulness. Even then it was enough to make me notice the shift in her attention.

II

Denise Levertov was born in Essex, England, in 1923, and lived there as a child. In her poem "A Map of the Western Part of the County of Essex in England" she says, in an obdurate tone: *and though I am a citizen of the United States and less a / stranger here than anywhere else, perhaps / I am Essex-born.*

Her inheritance was a rich re-working of Russian and Jewish and Welsh. Her father, Paul Levertoff, was descended from Shneour Zalman, a Russian founding father of the Habad branch of Hasidism. He converted to the Church of England and became an Anglican priest. Her Welsh mother, Beatrice Spooner-Jones, encouraged both literature and spirituality.

By her early thirties, however, she was living in America. This transit matters. She can be said to have come to the United States through marriage to the American writer Mitch Goodman. But her real passage there, what made her at home, came through the poetry of William Carlos Williams. She was not only domesticated by Williams. She was Americanized by him.

This also is important. Considering that Williams himself complained bitterly about the reverse transit of T. S. Eliot, there is something poignant and off-kilter about this return gift: a young woman looking to the States to unsettle her in almost the same way Eliot, as a young man, had looked to England to settle him. It provides a frame for Kenneth Rexroth's sharp, early comment on her in his review of *Here and Now*, her second book, in 1956: "In no time at all Denise came to talk like a mildly internationalized young woman living in New York but alive to all the life of speech in the country. Her verse changed abruptly. It would be easy to say it came under the influence of William Carlos Williams. It would be more true to say it moved into the mainstream of twentieth-century poetry."

III

Robert Duncan, Levertov's co-correspondent, held some sort of magic for his contemporaries. Many who knew him reported on his grace and intensity: "He taught as he spoke as he wrote," said Michael Palmer, "leading students on a wild, non-linear ride 'in search of the subject.'" He was much the same in personal conversation, insistently enthusiastic, combative, heuristic, making associational leaps and challenging you to follow across the open field and, at times, through the dark wood."

Duncan was born in 1919 in Oakland, California; his childhood was comfortable and strange. He was adopted by Bay Area Theosophists who accepted him after consulting charts and horoscopes. He went to Berkeley and studied English. By the 1940s he was fully engaged with the work of Gertrude Stein, Pound, Joyce and H.D. In the Bay Area his post-war presence was both crucial and defining.

In the fifties he built a community. He gathered around him Charles Olson, Robert Creeley and Denise Levertov. They became part of a loosely structured movement called the Black Mountain School of Poetry. It is a strange grouping, if it is a grouping at all. As poets, they are profoundly different from each other. Creeley and Levertov look to Williams. Duncan is nearer to the formal innovations of Pound. Nevertheless, Robert Creeley's editing of the *Black Mountain Review* between 1954 and 1957, as well as the glue of shared purposes and locations, made this grouping appear coherent. But not to everyone. In his *History of Modern Poetry* David Perkins writes somewhat sourly of the category: "They were widely known as the Black Mountain Poets, and though the name conveys no precise idea, it is now traditional and cannot be displaced."

Duncan's personal style—and it shows in these letters— was an alloy of arrogance and generosity. What's more he was didactic. He wanted to charm and scold the poetic energies around him into a shape he recognized. But the effort contained affection as well as control. It contained the extraordinary will to share a treasure of opinion, belief, faith, need and knowledge of the poetic process. His medium for doing this was first talk, then letters.

IV

The 1950s, when this correspondence begins, may well have been the transforming decade in twentieth-century poetry. Not even the twenties contained as many cross-currents. Nor, for that matter, the teens of the century, when Pound lit out for London and Eliot for Paris. In the fifties, the shared experiences of war, new media and economic expansion bound the English-speaking countries on both sides of the Atlantic into a new relation to language and self-perception.

When I was a young poet in Ireland this was already an era seen in a rearview mirror. It was looked at as golden, peaceful, productive. The last moment, perhaps, when poetry was central to society. When the sage and singer could still be coupled without irony.

But all was not well. This was the decade when the New Criticism was shown to be a salt in the wound of modernism. Critics like Cleanth Brooks and Blackmur formulated a forbidding outworks of comment. If anyone wondered how the voices of those fresh, talky, rebellious modernist poets, schooled in Paris, Berlin and London, who had quoted Laforgue and insulted the Georgians, had somehow modulated into the sonorous drone of earnest academic literary values, no one actually asked. Poetry was entering a new phase. Its traffic appeared be with a theory of itself which was more defining than defined.

One figure stood apart. From the beginning, William Carlos Williams had resisted the adventures of high modernism. While Eliot and Pound moved from London to Paris to Geneva, Williams was tunneling deeper into the adventure of Americanness. He wrote acerbically of Eliot and Pound's wistful flirtations with fragments of the past, stating that the Europeans would be surprised to see "parodies of the middle ages, Dante and *langue d'oc* foisted on them as the best in United States poetry."

More importantly, when Williams wrote in his *Autobiography* that *The Waste Land* "wiped out our world as surely as if an atom bomb had been dropped on it," he left undefined that phrase "our world." His stubborn independence made a space by which the undefined terrain of "our world" could be left for another poet to claim at a later date. And so it happened:

Williams's rancor and courage casts a long shadow over Levertov and Duncan's letters. Both revered him. But there is more to it than that. Williams's resistance to Eliot's strategies of high purpose and higher language opens a fault line in contemporary poetry. It is this line which makes the fifties so crucial a decade and this book so important a record. This is a turning point: the locus where the avant-garde separates from modernism.

Already the shape-shifting elements are coming into focus. A young woman able to adjust to a new context, but also—as the early letters show clearly—a new master. Here is the tinder for the later fire. The eloquence and waste of these letters can hardly be realized unless they are seen as less than an exchange between equals. They are also a wrenching allegory of an apprentice outgrowing an apprenticeship.

V

The charm of Denise Levertov's letters lies somewhere between a sideshow and a museum exhibit. That is to say, there is color and spectacle, but also the hush-making sight of something that will never be seen again. Never this exact grouping of poets. Never this particular throwaway intensity or epistolary energy.

When Duncan, for instance, is in London, he writes irrepressible notes about his existence there. He has just two hundred and fifty dollars left, he tells Levertov, and will have to go home. He could love London, but he has no money to love it with. He is going back to Mallorca where the living is cheap. Now we see Levertov arranging her New York Christmas with the paintings and poems sent by Duncan. Two years on and Duncan is writing from his home in Stinson Beach. The morning light is beginning. The cats are moving around. There is a rooster in the distance. And the sea is right there.

The rich, quirky details of their lives unreel page after page. This is a true friendship, the reader begins to feel. Here is a real meeting of talents. The letters are salted with praise, encouragement, consolation. Above all in a frank delight in each other's new poems.

But even here, even in this decade of the fifties, there is a warning of later tensions. Duncan writes that he is reading Pound. He is disappointed in his old master. There is a falseness there, he feels. "The feeling of what is false for me is the evident *use* of language to persuade." Here is the first warning shot. Art is an essence, an existence, a being for Duncan. It is not a set of purposes. But then the genial reasserts itself again: "I've a cold cup of coffee, a cigarette and a rainy day!" Duncan writes. "There's been a sheaf of letters from you. This clear direct line lifts me."

What is being shared here is important. It is nothing less than the rare process, not of poem-making, but of poet-making. Duncan's way of becoming a poet was essentially—as was Pound'—collaborative. He needed witnesses, companions, an audience. Levertov provides one. But she herself is more private and interior, more absorbed in craft at this stage. ("More and more I need a care for form in a poem for it to satisfy me.")

Levertov's correspondence reveals two poets caught in a moment. They are committed to process and not just product. Their intense exchanges make their respective poems happen at such close quarters that there is no time for artifice and distance. All this provides a remarkable record of a moment in American poetry when such a process promised a fresh start. In 1958 Duncan writes, "There's friendship and its courtesies—you're perhaps right that we've to deserve friendship. But love is nature to nature and your being is what sustains me there, not your deserving."

VI

So far so good. But the woman I met in the early eighties was hesitant and even disappointed when she spoke about the Black Mountain School. I found her retrospect strange and refreshing. It was a difficult moment in Ireland. The society, and its arts, were only beginning to creep forward from a harshly conservative view of women. I could not imagine wanting to belong to a largely male grouping as she had done. I must have said something of the sort to her, because I remember her reply. "I suppose in many ways," she said, "I was the token woman in the Black Mountain School."

And yet gender is only a fraction of these letters. What includes it and outpaces it is a formal disagreement which begins to grow from the early sixties. Not formal in the sense of individual poems. The formal tension comes in the construction and interpretation of the poet's responsibility.

It is a difference of more than style. Duncan believes in the imagination. He believes in the sacred space of the poem. He believes in an authority emanating from his own certainties which he considered binding on Levertov. Indeed, one of the places where this wandering epistolary adventure comes into sharp focus is in Levertov's growing restlessness as the Vietnam War takes hold. It appears to be a restlessness about the war. About the poem. About the career. But at its source, it is also a restlessness about Duncan's authority.

By the mid-sixties, although both are against the Vietnam War, there are intense, divisions between Duncan and Levertov. They are sharp and getting sharper. They are centered on what this life of imagination—this life they have been corresponding about for more than a decade—really means. In

July 1966 Levertov writes: "Then, I wanted (& want) to keep my participation in the Peace Movement (minimal though it is) in a *real* relation to my feelings—this seems to me terribly important—& part of that, I feel, is a matter of trying to grasp with the imagination what does happen in war."

The connection between war and imagination was essential to Levertov. But not to Duncan. By the end of 1968 Levertov had moved into committed activism. She was sending out letters. She was editing anti-war anthologies. Her life as a poet and her work as an activist became seamless entities. Would she have been warned or encouraged by Alicia Ostriker's clarifying comment?: "When I can't stand political and journalistic rhetoric any longer, I turn to poems. I don't believe poetry is therapeutic, but I do think it is diagnostic." During this time, Mitch Goodman, her husband, was arrested for his war-resistance activities. By the June of 1968 Duncan is writing her a troubled, complicated letter in favor of the individual conscience. His tone is still level. But he signals his deep unease with the coercive morality he senses in Levertov. "It is the sacrifice of your human individual lives," he writes to them both, "that you make in your convictions that so appalls me. It is like the carnage and destruction of lives in Vietnam." Later again he will try to silence her dissent with a chilling and memorable statement: "The poet's role is not to oppose evil, but to imagine it."

VII

The breaking point was Vietnam. The war swept them into passionate disagreement and a final rupture. In an unsent letter Levertov wrote, "Gradually my love for you dwindled."

But if the ruined friendship is the most poignant part of this correspondence, it is not the most interesting. The power of the letters comes from their canvassing of an old question. What responsibility has the poet in a time of violence? And can there be any definition of the imagination that could exempt a poet from such responsibilities? Duncan was a Romantic: the power of poetry, he suggested, lay in its freedoms. Levertov was a moralist: the power of poetry, for her, resided in its limits. For Duncan the glory of the poet was in knowing the reach of the aesthetic. For Levertov it lay in meeting the claims of conscience.

By the end of the correspondence there is a real sadness. Two decades of fellowship and sharing are scattered around, broken and irrecoverable. Several of the accusations are too bitter to be unsaid. Two wonderful poets have lost each other. Their separate witnesses—because they could not combine them—have become tainted.

Their stubbornness put me in mind of Heather McHugh's powerful poem "What He Thought." It describes a group of American writers on tour in Italy. On the last night of their visit they eat dinner in a family restaurant looking out on a public square and its statue. Someone asks, "What's poetry?" Suddenly, by way of answering the question, their host provides the story behind the statue. This is Giordano Bruno, a sixteenth-century Italian philosopher who contested the ideas of the Church. He was put to death in the square. The poem describes how, before his execution, he was silenced by an iron mask, for fear he would incite the crowd. "Poetry," the poem ends, "is what he thought but couldn't say."

McHugh's last line is a testament to the power of poetic witness: to that pure and passionate stance Levertov and Duncan lost. By the end of their correspondence, it is not poetry they are commending to each other but two rigid and separate interpretations of its history. Each in their way was a pure product of a nineteenth-century inheritance. The tragedy of their correspondence is not that they held one view, but that they could not listen to any other. The pity of the letters, and the waste of the negotiation they represented, is that Duncan and Levertov could have modeled a new and vital interpretation of the contemporary poem. But they missed the opportunity.

If anything can show the need for two maps, this marvelous dialogue which turned bitter is a clear example. Both Levertov and Duncan started out with one map. Levertov, whose views could have descended equally from Whitman or the Shelley of *The Masque of Anarchy*, believed in the ethical stance. Duncan was certain that the poem coerced into ethics and away from a private vision was equally at risk. They were not far apart. They could have met in the middle. But they failed to gauge the distance. And so a rich connection between private vision and a political stance eluded them, because they had no language for aligning the two.

As these poets struggle in their letters with the old, arduous concepts of conscience and craft they appear to be the last survivors on an island, waiting for rescue. In fact, they are that most poignant thing of all: two gifted people writing of an old art in a new medium. And steadily, letter by letter, moving towards the perfect misunderstanding.

Looking Back and Finding
Anne Bradstreet

I

found Anne Bradstreet first in a revealing context. That I found her at all is surprising. The names of American poets were not familiar when I was young in Ireland. Their work was largely unavailable in Dublin bookshops.

A few things got through: a random sampling of the excitements of elsewhere. One of these was *Homage to Mistress Bradstreet* by John Berryman. Published in 1953 in the *Partisan Review*—it came out as a single volume in 1956—it was a tour de force. It mixed eulogy and elegy. Its odd and vehement music made it more visible. Over the next decade the poem made its way into the conversations of young Irish poets. I was one of them.

For all that, I struggled with *Homage to Mistress Bradstreet*. To start with, it set out its stall in unfamiliar ways: with a rough, sinuous evocation of a snowy New England I had never seen. It was stubbornly mannered, hard to follow, given to cross-jumps of tone and point of view.

And yet my first information about Anne Bradstreet came from that poem. In the end, I didn't give it up. I continued to read. I floundered around in the richly divided identities of the piece. Part ode. Part dialogue. Part harangue. Part seance. And always the poet's voice, usurping the very identity he is seeking out: *thy eyes look to me mild.*

By the time the poem is over, Berryman has forced his way into the presence of Anne Bradstreet. The problem is, by the time the poem is over, we know how the Massachusetts winter drifts down through a broken syntax, how a scalding faith may once have sounded. We can even guess about John Berryman's need for a past, a source. But what do we know about her?

II

Anne Dudley was born in 1612, in Northamptonshire, in an England which had been nine years without its imperious queen. Post-Elizabethan England. Already sewing the whirlwind of the Civil War which was less than thirty years away. Already feeling the pinch and reproach of real-life Malvolios.

Her father was Thomas Dudley, at first clerk to Judge Nicolls in Northamptonshire, and then steward of the Earl of Lincoln's estate in Sempringham. These were not great people, but they lived in the shadow and peace of greatness. Although he himself had never been to university, he had been tutored by a graduate, and so he was able to give his daughter some knowledge of Greek and Latin and French.

It is hardly possible to imagine that England. It was a paradox, a contradiction. A place marching towards regicide and fratricide. It would live in Anne Bradstreet's memory, long after she left it. As John L'Heureux writes, in compelling lines from an early poem, "Being Born and a Few Consequences," *Some places come to mean so much: / never go back.* She never did go back. Yet there is no getting away from the fact that she was born in sight of the glories and upheavals of the Elizabethan Age. Then again, although as Anne Dudley she must have heard reminiscences of past glory, her reality was darker. She stood on a precipice of history. When the Massachusetts Bay Company was formed she was sixteen years of age. The year was 1628. Her father and Simon Bradstreet, her new husband, were founding members.

In 1630 the founding members began their "errand into the wilderness," as Samuel Danforth called it. The *Arbella* set sail from Southampton. Three months later, as John Winthrop wrote, *there came a smell off the shore like the smell of a garden.* They had made landfall. They were safe. They landed at Massachusetts. For Puritanism it was a new context. For America a new history. For Anne Bradstreet a new story.

Or half of one. As she steps onto the shore of New England, her old identity disappears. The young woman who loved England is lost in America. *I came into this country where I found a new world and new manners, at which my heart rose.* It is hard to imagine the discipline and restriction she must have faced. Not just the biting winter or the scarcity of food but an intellectual surrender the modern world has lost track of. Sometimes looking at her later work, it's possible to imagine she missed her old kingdom: "You're still there in the spectral impress," begins W. S. DiPiero in his poem "To My Old City." And so it must have been with the young Bradstreet.

No matter. Henceforth everything would be referred to

divine will: her life, her family, the death of children, the burning of her house. *It was not a scorpion I asked for, I asked for a fish, but / maybe God misheard my request,* writes Brigit Pegeen Kelly in her poem of will and revelation, "Iskandariya." From now on, Bradstreet lived entirely in the world of a hearing and mishearing God. It seemed everything must disappear into this.

Anne Bradstreet is that rare thing: a poet who is inseparable from history. It was history that swept her up. That took her from the graceful houses and prospects of Lincolnshire. And history again that brought her to the shores of Massachusetts. To use Elizabeth Tallent's title, "No One's a Mystery": events made Bradstreet visible.

The first winter was hard and hungry. Food was scarce. *Clams, and mussels, and ground nuts and acorns* must have seemed a poor diet after the feasts of Lincolnshire. Her father wrote the bleak truth back to England: *There is not a house where is not one dead, and some houses many.* Her life at that moment was set in a mold of survival and compliance. First the winter. Then a swift and relentless shifting. From Salem to Charlestown. To Cambridge. And finally to Andover. With each move, each a following on of her husband and father, she wrote herself deeper into that difficult history.

The mid-thirties found the Dudleys and Bradstreets living in Ipswich. They had a parcel of land. There was a gradual easing of the harsh conditions of their arrival. Now twenty-four years of age, with two children, Anne Bradstreet was established. She was raising her children. She was absorbing her landscape and writing in earnest. Now, for the first time, the advantages of her new location begin to be apparent.

Because Anne Bradstreet is a founding American poet, it is easy to forget that she was a dying star in the context of

European poetry. A poet writing against a background of adamant faith. A poet of a coterie—albeit a distinguished and faith-driven one—when the wider community was becoming fashionable. A poet whose inner and outer life remained powerfully undivided when such divisions were becoming the source of a new poetry in England.

The irony is, that had Anne Bradstreet stayed in England her artistic world would have been far less enabling. In a country with an approaching Civil War, a poisoned and politicized religious system, how would she have fared? The truth is she left a poetic tradition in which she might well have remained unregarded and founded another in which she is visible and central.

III

How do I see Anne Bradstreet? The answer is not simple. To start with, there is no figure in Irish poetry like her. To read of her travels, her pieties, the male power which surrounded her and to which she deferred, is to be surprised and unsettled. And then there is the complex act of reading itself. In Elizabeth Alexander's graceful words, from "Praise Song for the Day," *We encounter each other in words, words.* But time and distance also have an impact.

I never forgot when I read Bradstreet that I was an Irish woman poet watching an English woman become an American poet. I was not sure I should begin here—in the wonderful phrase of Susan Gubar and Sandra Gilbert—*to discover our grand, lost heritage of poetic presumption.* There was something layered and confusing about it all. But learning to listen to her plainspoken and resistant voice brought clarity. It made me more convinced than ever of some out-of-the-way poetic truths. Here is one of them:

There is a real fascination in the way poets of one time construct the poets of another. In the motivation with which a poet from the present goes to find one from the past. In an action which has the power to turn an orthodoxy into something less authoritarian: back from a set text into a living tradition.

But when we speak of the way a poet constructs the poets of another age, certain things get missed. When I was a young poet, it seemed to be an article of faith in the conversations around me that modernism was the watershed, the event which changed every poet's view of the recent and distant past.

I wasn't persuaded. I felt that the real watershed was more likely in the version of those centuries—the seventeenth and eighteenth—which were immediate intellectual possessions for the young poet. In those centuries, galaxies were found. Faiths were changed and diseases named. Those were the last continents of time where the hinterland of poetry lay as a gleaming, shining distance, still to be named and changed.

My version of those centuries is the Irish one. As Anne Bradstreet was seeking the New World, Ireland was losing the old one. As the Massachusetts Bay Colony was testing its ideas of grace, Ireland was sinking deeper into a realization of abandonment. As Simon Bradstreet was touching the light of manifest destiny, the bards and the unlucky chieftains of Ireland were preparing to learn the opposite. And what Anne Bradstreet took with her into her poetry, into the New World—that upward roll of Elizabethan music—is the very one that poisoned the wells for the Irish poets.

So when I picture her, this figure from the time and language which dispossessed mine, how can I see her clearly? I am not an American. I cannot be John Berryman, imagining her on the deck of the *Arbella*, founding his tradition.

And yet the truth is, I do see her. And somehow the fact that I do, seems to prove my point: that the reconstruction of poet by poet is independent of histories and boundaries. Besides, I cannot afford not to see Anne Bradstreet. She may not share my nation. But she adds to my world. She lays her claim, across every boundary, in spite of every distance. What's more, she tests my own powers of reconstruction. Pock-marked, slightly lame, outspoken and astonishing in her ability to survive the odds, she comes before me.

IV

Anne Bradstreet was thirty-eight when her poetry was published. Not in America, not in her native Massachusetts, but in an England she would never see again. Her brother-in-law, John Woodbridge, arranged it. He returned to England in 1850. He brought a manuscript of her poems with him and arranged for its publication. It is called *The Tenth Muse, Lately Sprung Up in America*.

This was Anne Bradstreet's only publication in her lifetime. Not until she had been dead six years did a second, amended edition of *The Tenth Muse* come out. A third followed in 1758. This is a leisurely publication schedule by any standards, and not until 1867 did John Harvard Ellis produce a scholarly and complete text of this book, with more authoritative inclusions.

In his "Epistle to the Reader" at the start of *The Tenth Muse,* Woodridge is quick to disclaim any poetic vanity on the part of his sister-in-law. He remarks that he has "presumed to bring to publick view what she [Bradstreet] resolved should in such manner never see the sun." Despite this, the poems are only occasionally successful. The public tone often falters, the language rarely shines. Only "In Honour of that High and Mighty Princess Elizabeth of Happy Memory" cracks open to suggest strength and craft. Despite a clumsy percussion, despite the rhymes swerving and chasing the sentiments around the page, there is a vigor of nostalgia here. And there is something compelling in this memory of a powerful woman put down on paper by a woman just learning her power:

> *Who was so good, so learn'd, so just, so wise*
> *From all the kings on earth she won the prize.*
> *Nor say I more than duly is her due,*
> *Millions will testify that this is true.*

One other poem catches the eye. It seems almost a modest addendum, coming at the end of *The Tenth Muse*. It is called "The Author to Her Book." It seems tucked away, having neither the breadth nor length of some of the other poems. But a second look will show it to be one of the truly remarkable poems of the seventeenth century.

To start with, it points forward to what will happen to Anne Bradstreet. After 1653, she clears her language of ornament. She rinses her tone. Now here she is, in preparation for that, making an *Ars Poetica*. A fresh, startling, unsettling statement. She uses the rough, domestic polemic which scalds her later poems. Her view of authorship is startling and transgressive: her book is a brat. It is an unwelcome and ugly child. It is plainly dressed. Suddenly the reader is included in a harsh and homely landscape—a place where mothers scrub their children, and feel the harsh weight of love. Suddenly the art of the Puritan world has a new and proper companion: the stripped-down and deeply felt life of a woman:

> *I washed thy face but more defects I saw*
> *And rubbing off a spot still made a flaw*
> *I stretched thy joints to make thee even feet,*
> *Yet still thou run'st more hobbling than is meet;*
> *In better dress to trim thee was my mind,*
> *But nought save homespun cloth i' th' house I find.*

As Anne Bradstreet's poems changed, her subjects closed in. Her father had died. Her feelings, her children, the life of her home, the spirit of her marriage—these became her themes. A different New England began to unfold. Now it was home—a shelter to the lives which had made it exist. We can imagine its life at last. Jorie Graham's lines, with their house-bound richness, from her poem "Soul Says" seem apt: *There as the fabric descends—the alphabet of ripenesses, / what is, what could have been.* The music shifted. The volume was turned down. The voice became more private and more intense. A quick-walking cadence accompanied the tone in which she told her story. In her poem to her husband, the sense of con-nection is exactly as found in Kenneth Fields's graceful lines from his epithalamium, "The Lovers' Community": *Today we see / The union of two souls, auras of what / Was, what is, what always has been.*

To My Dear and Loving Husband

> *If ever two were one, then surely we.*
> *If ever man were loved by wife, then thee;*

If ever wife was happy in a man,
Compare with me, ye women, if you can.

The work became blunt and appealing, gathering in accidents and turning them into designs. This poem, from the last year of her life, is deceptively simple. It describes her children; their arrivals and departures. Her images are deliberately anti-sublime. There is something slightly comedic in the figure of the bird calling after her fledglings. But in the context of seventeenth-century poetry the poem has a truculent freshness that is still surprising:

In Reference to Her Children, 23 June 1659

I had eight birds hatched in one nest,
Four cocks there were, and hens the rest.
I nursed them up with pain and care,
Nor cost, nor labour did I spare,
Till at the last they felt their wing,
Mounted the trees, and learned to sing;
Chief of the brood then took his flight
To regions far and left me quite.
My mournful chirps I after send,
Till he return, or I do end:
Leave not thy nest, thy dam and sire,
Fly back and sing amidst this choir.

Where did this voice, this fresh start on the world, come from? On the surface, it seems to be a woman crafting a dialogue with an authoritarian tradition. But whatever name is given to that authority—maleness or doctrine—the dialogue is sweetened by an objective irony. It appears the Puritan world could offer a woman poet more space for domestic detail and close-up dailiness than the Elizabethan. This is not to diminish the authorship: It is Anne Bradstreet's unique achievement that she could burrow into the crack and find a breathing space to be both a Puritan and a woman.

But the question remains—where exactly did that permission come from? Did she really find sustenance in a Puritan world for private and wilful expression? Could a culture of collective faith really nourish an individual imagination? The answer to that question—or answers—puts the most strain on the second subject of this piece: the relation between the past and present of poetry. Between the dead and living poet.

V

I wish I could see Anne Bradstreet clearly. I wish I could hold the pen she wrote with. I wish I could reach back to those first conversations in the Massachusetts colony. The fact is I can't. There are dangers to the contact between past and present poet. The poet of the present may invent the poet of the past in too facile a way.

Consider Anne Bradstreet. She is a compelling figure precisely because she stands outside the dialogue between past and present. Orthodox concepts of what is a public or a private poem will not work with her. A post-Romantic definition of what is the inner life and what is the outer—and who patrols the borders—will not work either.

The tense and elaborate world of poetry Anne Bradstreet left behind her must have seemed a faraway dream on the salty coasts of New England. But her shedding of that world is not immediately measurable. It would be a mistake to look for it in a single act of style. It has to be judged, like a quark or quasar, by absences.

The England which Anne Bradstreet left behind had already assigned a place to the poet. It is clearly marked in her poems in *The Tenth Muse* in which she echoes the place-making energies of the Elizabethan canon.

By the time Anne Bradstreet sailed for America, the English poet already had an inner and outer world. It had split apart the better to handle the intimate relation to power which history had ordained for that country. The outer world was coded into decorum and rhetoric there. The inner world was dark and raw.

What happened to Anne Bradstreet? To put it another way, what did not happen to her? To start with, she did not learn that the poet's place is necessarily in a split-apart world, as she might have if she had stayed in England. She learned something different. In her life and her work she enacted a high drama of the ordinary—of faith and dailiness and expression. In the process, the wound she might have lived with had she remained an English poet simply healed. And suddenly we have a woman in middle life who sees no need for a rift between faith, event and feeling. They are all one. She generates a poem in which they are indivisible from a sensibility which is not divided. And in so doing, changes the history of poetry.

By this interpretation, Anne Bradstreet wrote—in her best and later work—in a community so radicalized by change that the public and private were fused into one and the same. This is a rare circumstance for poetry. Nevertheless, her best poems were written in the heat of that fusion. They document a privacy that was public: they mark a public faith that was privately realized. If this is true, then the later shift into intimate poems about Bradstreet's domestic world are not true disruptions. They are continuations of a powerful intimacy between poet and community. Any of her later poems could be described by Mary Ruefle's words from her poem "The Letter": *Treat it as a bookmark / saving my place in our story.* Anne Bradstreet's best poems shine with the hard-won confidence of that complex historical self. They are excitingly innocent of the sense that this is a smaller life. By dismissing such definitions, she questions our own.

It would be wrong to make far-fetched claims for Anne Bradstreet. The work is memorable and strange. It can also be uneven, and underdeveloped in places. It would also be wrong to deny that she challenges our rights over the past. However powerful the relation between poet and past, it must always yield to a poet like her. Whose work comes from a world unwilling to be erased by our easy assumptions. Who makes it clear that any relation with her must be on her terms.

Reading Gwendolyn Brooks

I have never kept letters in any organized way. I put them aside. I stash them in drawers. I think I will come back to them. I rarely do. But I have kept one letter. By some mystery of adherence it has stayed with me since I first got it. I keep it as a reminder of what remains unsaid between poets.

The letter is from Gwendolyn Brooks. It was sent to me some years ago in a plain, hand-addressed envelope. Calling it a letter may be misleading. It is more a series of notes made on a letter I originally sent to her. It consists of my notepaper with a bold, added grid of comments. A line of her handwriting is ribboned across the top of the page. Two more are at the bottom. These notes—or more exactly statements—are written in a big-charactered script. They cross and re-cross the page in different-colored inks.

At the time I wrote to her I was editing an anthology with Mark Strand. It was published a year or so later under the title of *The Making of a Poem: A Norton Anthology of Poetic Forms*. It was an instructive task. The book concentrated, as the title pointed out, on poetic form and structure and was built on examples by various poets. Mark Strand was particularly illuminating about the forms he was dealing with and defining.

The sections of the anthology were divided so as to concentrate on different forms. Some of these were closed. Some were open. Some were genres, such as pastoral and elegy. One of the closed forms was the ballad. I was organizing this part of the book. The way the selection process worked, each section had a number of examples by other poets. The chapter was then closed with a discussion of a master poet, showcasing their work in this particular medium: celebrating their skill and concision.

I had one poem in mind, and one only, to finish the ballad section and provide an illustration of the balladeer's art. "Sadie and Maud" by Gwendolyn Brooks. It was first published in her 1945 volume *A Street in Bronzeville*. I had a deep admiration for her work. And so when I started to frame a section on the ballad I thought of her at once.

Permissions are always a concern in anthologies—both the expense and the availability. I was at Stanford, and acquiring them proceeded at a stately pace with the help of a gifted young poet, Nan Cohen. Most of the permissions came through agents and publishers.

Somewhere during the process I heard that Gwendolyn Brooks handled her own permissions. And so I wrote to her and the letter shows my handwriting on Stanford letterhead. I explained the anthology's purpose, and requested the permission. "The poem we have is 'Sadie and Maud,'" I wrote. Then I added, "I have loved your work since I was a young poet. I would be honored if you would give us permission and let us know your terms."

I wrote the letter and then forgot about it. I did not forget the poem. Nor the presence of Gwendolyn Brooks in the anthology. But the permission seemed a technicality, now slowed—as almost all the others were—to a glacial pace. It would fetch up somewhere, I was sure, as all the others had.

Time passed. The book was finished and submitted. And then, uncomfortably close to the last pass of the galleys, came this letter. The one I've managed to keep when so many others have been mislaid. It was my letter returned to me with writings and underlinings. Across the part of the page where I had written "The poem we have is 'Sadie and Maud'" Gwendolyn Brooks had placed a glowing, insistent underline in red ballpoint. "Too simplistic to represent my entire output," the words above it read.

At the top of the page, in another band of script, she wrote, "Thanks for the praise." At the bottom, again in red ink, she wrote, "How about samples suggested on back of this letter?" When I turned the page over there was a list including "Lovers of the Poor," "We Real Cool," "The Sundays of Satin-Legs Smith," "Bronzeville Mother Loiters in Mississippi," as well as some others. And then at the very bottom of the page she had added, "Accept any of them for free!"

For a moment I was wistful. For a moment I wondered if I should write to her again. "Sadie and Maud" did not of course define her achievement. Nor had we intended it should. But it helped to define the contemporary ballad. Its bleak re-working of the relation with audience, its shifting of the stance of the balladeer added an innovative dimension, scalding an old form with new ironies. My wistfulness extended to the headnote I had written which would now never see the light of day. I re-read it with a sense of regret:

"'Sadie and Maud' is witty and entertaining, despite its

darkness. It conveys the power of the ballad in a contemporary context, disguising a sharp and public tone with deceptively musical cadences. No one, however, reading the poem again, could doubt the passionate engagement of the balladeer. The short lines become daggers of irony, examining the popular expectations of what is right and decorous for young women—what goals they should have, what roles they should undertake. The daring Sadie and the cautious Maud are played off against each other in these brief, jumpy stanzas, like figures in a fairy tale. And the moral, as so often in the fable or the nursery rhyme, is clear: Personal risk is rewarded. Society is obliquely punished. The poem reminds us that the role of the balladeer in our times can also be moral and satirical; that beneath the entertainment, the balladeer can make a secret and disturbing claim on the reader."

But the hesitation lasted only a moment. Apart from the matter of legal copyright, any editor or co-editor would have wanted to change this simply because it was Gwendolyn Brooks's wish. "We Real Cool" had been a second, off-kilter choice for the ballad section. With the help of my editor, Jill Bialosky, who, as a poet herself, had patience with the request, it was changed—although not without some difficulty, considering the late stage of the proofs. I re-wrote the section. I re-routed the argument on the ballad through "We Real Cool." I wrote to inform Gwendolyn Brooks of the decision and the permission was forthcoming.

And then I took the letter and put it away. Its interest for me, in an objective sense, was the insight it provided into an extraordinary poet editing her own work, her own legacy in the moment. In that broader sense, Brooks's argument that "Sadie and Maud" was "too simplistic" was justified. In the narrow terms of the anthology—which was focused on poetic form—perhaps not.

In the subjective sense it was a lost opportunity. I wrote to Gwendolyn Brooks in 1999. She died the following year. The letter represents the broken, thwarted conversation that can exist—that often has existed—between poetic generations. I had managed in the exchange to allow everything to elude me. Writing as an editor requesting a permission, I managed to say almost nothing I wanted to say. I conveyed not one word of substance to a poet who mattered to me. I missed the chance to tell her in detail that one of the poems she offered on the back of the letter—"The Sundays of Satin-Legs Smith"—came like "Sadie and Maud" from a book to which I owed a great deal. *A Street in Bronzeville.*

Perhaps the reason I missed the opportunity was because of an element of confusion. In any description of influence and affinity, the story needs to be clear. This one was not. What was unclear was not my journey as a poet; but my journey towards her work.

Perhaps I hesitated because of an inherent awkwardness. Gwendolyn Brooks had inspired me with a book written out of a powerful history. I engaged the book. I read it and re-read it. But as a young poet in another country, I escaped that history. And so I came to be painfully conscious that I was not in Brooks's world.

To start with, I was white and middle-class. I lived in another suburb far removed from hers. There was no real point of contact between the small, quiet suburb of Dundrum in 1970s Dublin and the South Side of Chicago in the 1940s. The poems in *A Street in Bronzeville* are shadowed by their political moment. They lay down a language of anger as well as music, of outrage as well as joy in their characters and interiors. I know now I comprehended only a fraction of the narrative of race and injustice which *A Street in Bronzeville* suggests. What I knew came to me through my reading; and my reading was without context.

And yet I came from a nation where the memory of colony intruded on speech and memory. I lived in a country where the exclusion of women was an everyday reality. If this grand-daughter of a runaway slave, already a mother at twenty-three, stood at an intersection of history and poetry I could not see, I could still sense her poise and courage. And if I had only an incomplete insight into the confluence of race, history and lyric craft which made her first volume almost an insurgency in its time, I never felt I would or should be beyond reach of her voice. If I could not, in historical or political terms, be her witness, I could still be her reader.

I certainly loved the book. Even the name of it—*A Street in Bronzeville*—had a particular charm and meaning. Its obstinately local title refers to an area described later by Brooks as "about forty blocks" running north and south of Chicago from Nineteenth to Sixty-ninth Street. When I opened the book all those years ago, I took courage from its insistence on the neighborly. I was beginning to have a sense of the theater of ordinary life. I was starting to write about my own suburb. But I was still shy about putting it into my work, still timid as to how much of it should be included in a poem. Now here was a whole suburb, exuberantly recorded by a woman who was only a year or two older than me when she wrote it down.

Today I see more clearly what I found in Brooks and what I missed. Rita Dove describes her first reaction, at seventeen, to reading her: "The poems of Gwendolyn Brooks leapt off the

pages of the book in my hands and struck me like a thunder-
bolt. These were words that spoke straight from the turbulent
center of life."

I had less insight. And yet in my first reading it was the
sheer reach of *A Street in Bronzeville* that charmed and dazzled.
It was a voice in poem after poem, room after room, saying
Look at this, remember this. No one else had come from the mix
of the trivial and important which a suburb provides to do this
in such a confident way.

In a 1961 interview with Studs Terkel, Brooks revisited
her vivid characterizations. "I was just interested in putting
people down on paper," she said. In the poems, she views
women and men—Sadie and Satin-Legs Smith—with equal
interest and an intense involvement. In Carol Ann Duffy's
poem "Warming Her Pearls," the speaker of the poem writes
about her obsession with her mistress. "I see her every movement in my head," she says. All the movements of the characters in *A Street in Bronzeville* have been seen in Gwendolyn
Brooks's head.

From the standpoint of lyric inclusion this was exemplary.
The book is a panorama. Images are stitched together into an
encompassing narrative: Over here, someone is having their
hair put up. Over there, someone else is looking out the window in the late sun. Now there is another person crossing
over to the southwest corner of a room where there is an
ink-spotted table on which Sunday dinner will be served. It is
going to be chicken and rice or chicken and noodles.

This is an affectionately observed world. It may not, for
instance, cast as long a shadow as the wrenching lines of
Helene Johnson, in "A Missionary Brings a Young Native to
America." When Johnson writes of how *A belt / Of alien tenets
choked the songs that surged / Within her,* there is a pause, a

disruption to those lines. Place is portrayed—with every rea-son—as hostile to imaginative life.

But not here. *A Street in Bronzeville* is a model of obser-vation. "I wrote about what I saw and heard in the street," Brooks stated in her autobiographical *Report from Part One*. "I lived in a small second-floor apartment at the corner, and I could look first on one side and then on the other. There was my material." And the material is assembled over and over again: Now from another side of the panorama comes the sound of a "big cheap radio." And in yet another section a man goes to Joe's Eats, a man who is described as walking "powerfully alone." Towards the end of the book, there are soldiers—"gay chaps"—at the bar, ordering drinks, making merry in the aftermath of war. And yet one of them says, "I swear to keep the dead upon my mind."

There are many charms to *A Street in Bronzeville*. But what struck me first and influenced me most was its imagizing of narrative. This swiveling of the head and turning of the eyes in poem after poem so that the reader is forced, over and over again, to stand aside and move to a different location. There are no comfort zones here. No static observation platforms. Everything is shifting and moving, as though on deck at sea.

The result is a closing in, a wearing down of a conventional stance. Finally the reader is drawn into a powerful and unset-tling intimacy: is made open to questions which are equal parts old-fashioned balladeering and unsettling, Prufrock-type rhetoric. One of the clearest examples is called "Kitchenette Building." It is a cropped sonnet, a thirteen-line word-portrait of claustrophobia and resignation, with a sharp moment of resistance. The poems begins accepting the limitations of cramped space.

We are things of dry hours and the involuntary plan,
Grayed in, and gray. "Dream" mate, a giddy sound, not strong
Like "rent," "feeding a wife," "satisfying a man."

The craft aspects are tightly woven. Marilyn Hacker's perceptive comment on another of Brooks's books, *Annie Allen*, is also true of the poetry here. "Brooks's choice of a tightly metered and pyrotechnically rhymed form in constant tension with her verbal exuberance adds both irony and constant musical tension." The outcome in this poem is that finally the reader stands—or at least I did—as both reader and neighbor right there in the corridor, inhaling the cooking scents, listening to the sounds of the day ending:

> *But could a dream sent up through onion fumes*
> *Its white and violet, fight with fried potatoes*
> *And yesterday's garbage ripening in the hall,*
> *Flutter, or sing an aria down these rooms,*
>
> *Even if we were willing to let it in,*
> *Had time to warm it, keep it very clean,*
> *Anticipate a message, let it begin?*

And then, just as a dream ghosts its way into the cooking steam, the choked corridors, a fall-to-earth practicality comes back. *We think of lukewarm water, hope to get in it.* That is how the poem ends. And we are shaken about in these small spaces, and made intimates of the contradictions of longing for another reality and still keeping a sharp eye on the hot water. It is a consummate miniature of neighborhood, one of the many that works its magic in the book.

We wonder. But not well! Not for a minute!
Since Number Five is out of the bathroom now,
We think of lukewarm water, hope to get in it.
("Kitchenette Building")

I still own my edition of *A Street in Bronzeville*. It is a small, finely printed book with an orange stripe across the top. In the photos of the time, a smiling Gwendolyn Brooks holds the book with its original cover—which is an image of a brick wall. But nothing seemed walled or dark about the book when I first read it. On the contrary it had a heart-lifting energy. I wanted to be able to write about a suburb with that detail, that boldness. I understood that though I could not claim insight into her terrible history, her imagination of it had been so intense, that I would be allowed to share in the outcome, if not the origin. That this was how poetry worked; how it reached across boundaries.

I also recognized that the Dublin neighborhood I lived in bore no resemblance at all to Bronzeville. My street was quiet. My neighbors were involved, as I was, in the small events of a day: a car backing out of the drive in the morning, a child returning from school in the afternoon. No marvelous and troubling appearance was made there by Satin-Legs Smith. The demographic we belonged to was far easier, even though it was beginning to be shadowed—as everything was in Ireland then—by the violence in the North and the repression of truth in the South.

And yet—for all its unlikeness—I turned in this Dublin suburb to a faraway Chicago street and its poet for a permission I was lacking. It was not the only book I looked to at that time. But it stayed with me in a particular way. I read it with the knowledge I had; I re-read it with the insights I lacked.

I first interpreted *A Street in Bronzeville* as a continuation of the imagery of urban life. I saw it adding to a tradition laid down by the poems of Langston Hughes and T. S. Eliot and Carl Sandburg and Hart Crane. Now that tradition had come to Brooks. I saw the book as part of the body of work that portrayed the city as both a desolate place and an inevitable theater of humanity.

Today that first reading seems incomplete. If *A Street in Bronzeville* is a nuanced reading of a place, it is also a powerful critique of race and nation. The critic George E. Kent wrote, "Gwendolyn Brooks shares with Langston Hughes the achievement of being responsive to turbulent changes in the black community's vision of itself and to the changing forms of its vibrations during decades of rapid change." The figures I admired so much in the book—Satin-Legs Smith and Sadie— were vivid images. But they were also rooted ones. They grew down into a tragic history. I sensed their power and yet I missed, at least on a first reading, the exact meaning of that descent. Even after I understood the history more I continued to lose the nuances, much as I think a non-Irish reader might miss the meaning of a poem on the Irish Famine. There are fractions of reference that cannot be conveyed to someone who has not been constructed by the same elements as have constructed the poem.

And yet this can also be a half-truth. Understanding Brooks more fully became an act of negotiation rather than affinity. The African-American references in the book I could not presume to understand were translated into Irish colonial angers I did. But it was a fragile transposition.

But always I came back to the same place, to the same book. It seemed appropriate now and then to wonder what histories were present in a poem and missing in a reader. But those thoughts vanished as soon as I picked up the slight volume again, with its surprisingly thick pages—considering the post-war era—and its elegant print, described at the back as Linotype Bodoni. As soon as I began to read the musical stanzas, with their vivid reports of character and neighborhood, I remembered again why I believed *A Street in Bronzeville* was a profoundly inclusive text. And why I never believed that any poet would want a reader banished from a poem's imaginative power because they lacked access to the history that gave rise to it.

In the days when I first read *A Street in Bronzeville* I lived close to the life of my own street. It was on the edges of Dublin; a new migrant in a modestly growing economy: a place thrown up almost overnight with houses and streetlamps, and no memories. Unlike the voices and faces in *A Street in Bronzeville*, I shared no history with my neighbors. The only one we had in common was the history we were making every day with our small actions. Eventually that would be my subject.

As I drove children to school in the morning, or came back to the house at night, I could perhaps have argued that I saw Gwendolyn Brooks's vivid cast of characters—so deep an impression had they made—adding color and meaning to where I lived. But I didn't. No Sadie and Maud. No Hattie Scott at the end of the day. What I felt was something different: a powerful encouragement to find my own meaning. A prompt to name my own neighborly world.

Being an Irish Poet:
The Communal Art of Paula Meehan

I

Between 1900 and 1950 Irish poetry was tempered by far-reaching change. A new state. A lexicon of freedoms. A different role for Irish writing. Under these pressures, literature in Ireland re-defined itself. The excitement of those years pushed Irish poetry in new directions. Yeats, Patrick Kavanagh, Louis MacNeice, Denis Devlin—all, in various ways and with various degrees of success, responded to the challenge.

Yet, with few exceptions, women were not part of this. One of the reasons may be that their relation to the new nation was complicated and ambiguous. As indeed it was to the literary tradition. The apparent end of colony in Ireland left women with new laws, new strictures and, unfortunately, new silences. In a very specific way, as far as women were concerned, shadows of colony remained.

"When the soul of a man is born in this country there are nets flung at it to hold it back from flight." Stephen Dedalus's exasperated comment, with a shift of gender, is especially applicable. Irish society was suspicious of the possible association between the concepts of woman and poet: between a category as indulgently defined as the individual artist and one so narrowly and tensely construed as a woman's identity.

The effects of this exclusion were significant. Many fine poems were written; many changes were reflected in them. But the lack of the voice and vision of women left certain elements of Irish poetry static, unchallenged. The old association between the public and political poem remained in place. It was a nineteenth-century inscription—something deep in the Irish poem.

The reverse is also true. The emergence of women has now made a new space in the Irish poem. The detail and ordinariness of a woman's life in Ireland—the very source of suspicion at one time—has become a powerful lens on the reality of the state. In the work of women poets the so-called domestic shifts the political poem into a private realm where priorities are re-arranged. The old registers of power and rhetoric remain. But a new vocabulary of sense and impression has been admitted.

In her path-breaking book on women's poetry, *Stealing the Language*, Alicia Ostriker advocated that women poets needed to be "thieves of language." And so it has turned out. This is just one of the strategies by which women's poetry has come to the center of Irish poetry: where it re-writes and re-claims and adds immeasurably to the past.

It took time for this to happen. I remember those publications by women poets which seemed a tectonic shift. I felt it with Medbh McGuckian's *Flower Master*, published in 1982. Its bold re-arrangements of language and image brought energy to everything. When Eiléan Ní Chuilleanáin's *The Magdalene Sermon and Earlier Poems* was published I was captivated by the mythic image of a stone woman: "A green leaf of language comes twisting out of her mouth." Nuala Ní Dhomhnaill's poems, as published and translated, produced a constant reference system of wit and revision and lyric ingenuity. I also sensed it when I received a single volume in the post one spring morning. It was by Paula Meehan.

II

The first time I opened *The Man Who Was Marked by Winter* I marveled at the structure. I had known Paula Meehan's work for years. I had owned *Return and No Blame* since 1984 and *Reading the Sky* since 1985. I had even read with her in the mid-eighties in Dublin. Not that much of the occasion remains. My memory of it blurs into a crowded room in Buswells Hotel, a thin silvering of mist on the glass doors.

What we said that evening is gone. But the conversation between poets continues in surprising ways. And so it was that I was holding the bright covers of her new book in the upstairs room where I worked in Dublin. It was early summer, 1991. The wild yellows of the laburnum outside made an improbable background to the crimson endpapers. I stood there, in that triangle of color, trying to clarify my impressions.

I had recently seen a television documentary on the New York School of painters. It was almost a home movie, a wandering journal of memories and questions. One of them stuck. Why, said one of the painters—I am paraphrasing at this distance—should a canvas be confined? Why should it accept the context of its space? Why should a painter consent to the predetermined limit of a rectangle?

Now here I was looking at poems which seemed to resist their confinement on the page. Each piece was fluid rather than framed, ready to spill into the next. Poems like "The Pattern," with its tough meditation on inheritance, reached into other pieces, such as "The Statue of the Virgin at Granard Speaks." The constant shifting of image to theme and theme to address was made possible by the strength of the voice. It was clear and compelling. It had a timbre that held tight the argument and let loose the meaning.

"It is hard to even begin to gauge how much a complication of possessions, the notions of 'my and mine,' stand between us and a true, clear, liberated way of seeing the world." These words by Gary Snyder—a guiding spirit for Meehan—were written against mid-century American materialism.

They are also apt for this poetry. The sociable nature of these poems, their resistance to Snyder's narrow definition of "my and mine," is arrived at with confidence. I immediately felt, on reading them, a difference in voice and posture. These poems reached out. They implied community, even while recognizing its flawed and problematic nature.

One of the strongest examples of this is "Two Buck Tim from Timbuctoo." The poem, with its unlikely title, comes near the start of the book. It describes the speaker taking in an old 78 record, found at the back of the house under rubble. The record is brought inside the cottage and played.

Then, as in so many poems in this book, the conventional narrative comes to a dead stop. The action unfolds jerkily, through movie-like stills, into a theater of gestures and regrets. Surreal apprehensions dance around the theme as it

attempts a re-creation of the tragedy of flight from the land.
American music. Irish emigration.

> *Ghosts of the long dead*
> *flocked from their narrow grooves beneath foreign soils*
> *to foxtrot around my kitchen in the dusk.*

This, to return to Snyder's words, is not built on any notion
of "my and mine." This is about what is *ours*. Or what used
to be.

There were other poems I immediately admired. "Ard
Fheis." "My Love About His Business in the Barn." And, especially, "Buying Winkles" for its precise and genial details: The
little night skies of the winkles. The pin that coaxed them
out in all their sweetness. *Tell yer Ma I picked them fresh this
morning.* In these pieces I saw both poet and playwright. In
fact, right through the book, I recognized an alloy of drama
and lyric.

I admired the book. But I was also, in some way, unsettled. This was the start of the nineties: a time of upheaval
and reflection in Irish poetry. Women were publishing more
and being challenged more. There was a stir of change in the
country itself. The peace process was just over the horizon.
The ideas and energies which would eventually form a new
direction were in the air.

The old surfaces on which I had rested as a poet were
breaking up. I seemed to be arguing with myself most the
time. I found it impossible to keep the process pure. Everything I read, every new poem, entered it. *The Man Who Was
Marked by Winter* took its position there too.

It was all about poetry, this argument. About the political

poem and also—seen from another angle—about what ratio of the public and private selves should go into it. No matter how I tried, I found it hard to settle the question in my own mind. The Meehan poems I was looking at were fresh witnesses.

The Ireland of the 1980s—the decade from which the poems in *The Man Who Was Marked by Winter* come—was a quicksand for an Irish poet. No ground was safe; no assumption was solid. I experienced that time as a harassment of familiar lyric categories. The need to weigh my life as a woman in language; the continual violence in the North; the sense of familiar poetic categories disintegrating—all of it made for a continual revising of ideas and beliefs.

But it was more than that. Although I lived in Ireland, and wrote there, I belonged to a generation which had seen the poem become a migrant; its aesthetic constantly being revised by other countries. In fact, Paula Meehan was already in this new terrain, finding sustenance in faraway cultures and other poetries.

As I stood in my workroom on the very edge of summer, with the *Man Who Was Marked by Winter*, that was what I was looking at: a poem shaken by the local but shaped by a wider aesthetic. The public poem. The political poem. I had come to think of this manifestation of the art as often trapped between two words. Always governed by dark twin stars: the words, the stars, being *we* and *I*.

The *I* is simply explained. It is relatively stable. It is the *I* of Tennyson's "Charge of the Light Brigade." The *I* of Oscar Wilde's "Ballad of Reading Gaol." Of Denise Levertov's "Tenebrae." Of Whitman's "When Lilacs Once in the Doorway Bloomed." Of Yeats's "The Fisherman." The *I* that signals a poet is in and of their time.

The *we* is a different matter. The *we* implies community, shared assumptions, an unshaken compact between poet and audience. The *we*—whatever is suggested by that pronoun in the political poem—is transitional from age to age. It shimmers and re-states itself. For the political poet the *we* is always volatile—one minute stable, the next vanishing. For the reader, going back to the poem of an earlier moment, the *we* can become downright illegible. A hundred years later, or even a decade, the reader is free to say about that *we*—*I don't get it* or *It feels so dated*. At any time—through change and history—the pronoun can desert the poem, the poet and the reader.

It had deserted me. I no longer wrote it. I had stopped looking for it. Whereas at the start of the eighties, in a poem I wrote then, called "The Emigrant Irish," I had freely written *we need them* and *we put them out the back*, now things felt diferent. As the decade wore on in Ireland—hearing news of violence, weighing political double-talk, watching a toxic social stasis continue where women were concerned—there seemed less and less possibility of a *we*. In the Ireland of the time—or so it seemed to me—the pronoun had fractured into pieces.

And yet here it was, restored in a book I was holding on a summer evening. The *we* implied by "The Pattern" or "The Statue of the Virgin at Granard Speaks" or "Buying Winkles" seemed immediately different—more whole, more healed— than any I could have used. What's more, it was not a *we* that was oppositional, highlighted by separation from the *I* as often happens in the political poem. I had managed the political poem by making a deliberate distance between the two pronouns, framing the speaker in the tension. Paula Meehan was doing the opposite. In her poems, the *we* had ceased to be merely political.

It had become communal. Far from being oppositional to the *I*, it was integral.

And no wonder. The communities, like the pronouns in Paula Meehan's poems, are not separable. They are bound together. The *we* is not only communal. It is the community the *I* has grown from *and will not abandon*. The poems in the book remind the reader at every turn of that interdependence. And I, as a reader, who had not seen this for a long time, was moved and restored by it.

This is particularly true of "The Pattern," a poem about generation. To start with, this is not a conventional landscape. The figures are awry. There is something skewed, off-balance about it all. A daughter looks back at her mother's life through a lens of grief and language. What is remarkable is how the private and secret life of a woman is balanced in the poem with the public interrogations of the speaker. The mother's is a hidden, afflicted world. The poem does not try to drag it to the light. But the technical ease with which the speaker of the poem moves from private grief to public reference sets the tone:

> Little has come down to me of hers,
> a sewing machine, a wedding band,
> a clutch of photos, the sting of her hand
> across my face

What is compelling here is the harsh inventory of inheritance—but not just that. Also the way that the background and foreground of the Irish poem—so often full of conventional perspective—are collapsed so that the location is discoverable in the person, and not the other way around. The

city is hardly mentioned and yet the Dublin of harsh colors
and hard lives is made powerfully available:

> *And as she buffed the wax to a high shine*
> *did she catch her own face coming clear?*
> *Did she net a glimmer of her true self?*

"The Pattern" opens a new space. Into it comes that light
of real lives—of women and their daughters caught in the
strange and contradictory zone of colony. But it also models
a different kind of communal poem. The mother and daughter are contrary, but not divided. The speaker of the poem is
imaginatively released and not stifled.

> *I was sizing*
> *up the world beyond our flat patch by patch*

In my first reading of *The Man Who Was Marked by Winter*,
looking at the gathering of the political into the communal,
it felt right to take the book as text. But as time went on, it felt
equally important to try and locate its context.

The 1980s in Ireland—this is a simplified version—seemed
like a decade of endless talk. No doubt because of the sprawl-
ing political conversation, poetry was often forced into a corrective posture. Increasingly, in the work of that decade, there
was an emphasis on a meticulous poetic self. Books like *The
Hunt by Night* by Derek Mahon, published in 1982, insisted on
a scrupulous and solitary viewpoint. The poems in his book
which pointed towards the Northern violence were wistful
and oblique. The political poem, Mahon's work seemed to
advocate, should have more undertones than tones.

It was understandable that the poem turned inward. The public conversation, whether about Ireland, politics, violence or women was often coarse and exigent. Deaths became statistics; participants became actors. The poem offered a place where, to quote Mahon, "a thought might grow." The nuanced self of this sort of poem was a refreshing answer that seemed to imply a question. How could a poetic self thrive and grow at that time unless sheltered by a fastidious withdrawal? It seemed that the solution was to increase the privacy as an antidote to the public noise.

Something very different, however, is happening in "The Statue of the Virgin at Granard Speaks." It breaks with the decade. It also overturned many of my own perceptions about where the speaker needed to be in the poem. This spacious narrative, with its tense polemic and scalding argument, is an eye-catching part of the book—and indeed of all Meehan's work.

The speaker is an *I*. Is, in fact, the Virgin Mary. The edginess of her small talk, her intense arguments, have the opposite effect to "The Hunt by Night." This *I* turns the reader immediately into a *we*—into an historic community, a receptive register for worn-out loyalties and disturbed religious feeling. The poem describes a young girl who lies down in front of a statue of the Virgin Mary in a grotto and gives birth to her child. Both mother and child die there. The desolation of the event evolves into a critique of the hypocrisy of a society.

> *They kneel before me and their prayers*
> *fly up like sparks from a bonfire*
> *that blaze a moment, then wink out.*

Even with its ironies, this poem speaks to a shared world. What goes deeper here than any pronoun, is an alchemy between private and public: between the singular voice of the Virgin and a reader growing more communal, more drawn in, with every line. The voice of the Virgin addresses a lost unity. But even in the moment of loss, what is shared is remembered; what is lost is recognized. The reader becomes a participant in both memory and recognition.

> *On a night like this I remember the child*
> *who came with fifteen summers to her name,*
> *and she lay down alone at my feet*
> *without midwife or doctor or friend to hold her hand*
> *and she pushed her secret out into the night,*
> *far from the town tucked up in little scandals,*
> *bargains struck, words broken, prayers, promises,*
> *and though she cried out to me in extremis*
> *I did not move,*
> *I didn't lift a finger to help her*

"Talk to me of originality and I will turn on you with rage. I am a crowd, I am a lonely man, I am nothing." Yeats's paradigm of formal distance, which includes this sentence, is just one example of a different approach to constructing a poetic self. And there are many others. Irish poetry has never had just one script.

The problem lies in weighing the gains and losses. The private perspective can often make the best political poem: the painful outsiderism lifting a complex situation to the light. But the privacy can also be a barrier to the inclusion of the reader. Paula Meehan's poems in *The Man Who Was Marked by Winter* choose not to retreat into a private shelter. *Look at me*, they seem to say to a reader, *your world is not lost here.*

Of course, this traffic between public and private was not

new to Irish poetry. The issues raised by the book fitted with others I had come upon. It reminded me of some of my first reading of contemporary Irish poetry, when I was a student at Trinity. Looking back, I remembered encountering echoes and instances of what I felt now. Patrick Kavanagh's "In Memory of My Mother," for instance, was a case in point. With its elegant, open-hearted lament for a shared world, it also had once seemed a celebration of community, as well as a record of loss.

Kavanagh's poem to his mother holds a mirror up to "The Pattern." Both commend the idea that ties of community can be inventories of the imagination. In the same way, there is an anger, an edge to *The Great Hunger* that fits with the obstinate, anti-authoritarian polemic of "The Statue of the Virgin at Granard Speaks."

But there are also reversals to the communal which hold clues to this book. During the sixties, Thomas Kinsella— another Dublin poet—was doing exactly what the speaker in "The Pattern" narrates—*fitting each surprising / city street to city square to diamond*. His work, however, describes an oppositional arc to Meehan's, moving from the often communal poetry of "Another September," with its windfalls, country gardens and lyric geniality to the hermetic fury of "Notes from the Land of the Dead."

When I asked myself what happened to the dialogue between individual and communal voices in our poetry, and why it seemed to drop out of sight, I blamed its absence on that strange decade of the 1980s. New pressures had been created. New expectations had been raised. Northern Irish poetry had demonstrated how a poetry could be conscripted by history. Michael Longley and Seamus Heaney had written essential political poems. But the template was the older one—a private speaker lifting a public reality to the light by defining a distance from it. A communal vision had little play in this. And almost no possibility of existing within it.

Once the dialogue re-appears, it can be seen reaching further back again. In Yeats's poem "The People," the speaker inveighs against a community that had little interest or respect for a poet's work. The speaker rants against the neglect. But then his "Phoenix" replies: *never have I, now nor any time / Complained of the people.* When the poem ends, the speaker is ashamed, re-instated in the tensions and necessity of a conversation with community—*I sink my head abashed.*

And so, that early summer day, I felt a new excitement. Not only did it seem to me that *The Man Who Was Marked by Winter* added iconic poems—"The Pattern," "The Statue of the Virgin at Granard Speaks"—to an Irish canon which needed them. The book also re-stated that inclusive *we*, which had been thwarted in Irish poetry. By doing this, Paula Meehan took up important unfinished business. By extending its reach and significance, she made it visible again.

A Latin Poet: A Lost Encounter

I

Ilearned Latin the hard way. As an over-and-done-with discipline. A house of correction for all the slipshod habits of thought Anglo-Saxon had induced. As a schoolgirl, bent over the small underlined paperbacks of Horace and Virgil, I came to think of the Roman poets—all men of course—as torso-less heads in a temple: robust, accusing, authoritative and long gone.

I was not a willing student. I chewed my pencil, stumbled over unseens, sat for hours with Arnold's grammar and dreaded tests. I was seventeen. Since I did not speak Irish, having spent my childhood away, I had to sit the British GCSE exams which were accepted by Trinity College. I chose Latin and English. It was all I was able for and to begin with I doubted my choice. My small, elderly Latin teacher was apple-cheeked and angry. She smoked constantly. She alternately glared and shouted.

She was also—although it took time to see this—a remarkable teacher. She had little enough interest in me as a student. But for Latin, she had an infinite passion. The first circumstance became surprisingly unimportant to me. Because of the second, I gained a lasting sense of linguistic adventure. Her passion for syntax, her pride in the turn-on-a-sixpence neatness of certain constructs eventually got through.

Seasons passed under the window. The exams came nearer. I began to see the wonder more than the grind. I started to understand that the words on the page—previously just instruments of my humiliation—could be monuments of concision. How the time transport of the ablative absolute and the magical compressions of the gerund re-structured time. I began to realize that this dialect of logical kingdoms and temporal solutions was different from anything else I had known.

What I gained was profound. What I missed was essential. I had little enough sense of irony. As I sat learning Tacitus, the sea behind me circled around one of the few islands in Europe which had never been a Roman colony. The power of compression and grammar I was learning would be questionable gifts for my chosen future as a poet. The power of history enacted through the destiny of a language was an inaccurate text for understanding my own country. Irish literature, I would find, had succeeded through an opposite strategy: by taking the language of power and forcing it to tell the Irish story of injury and oppression.

And there was more. I knew that Latin had a past. I had no idea it had a future. I had no sense of the sinuous history of the language, weaving in and out of European courts in the Middle Ages. Being assumed and resumed in the writing of poets for whom it was not a first language but a learned survival.

Had I known, as I sat over my primer, that the language

I was struggling with had such a future I would have been taken aback. Had I been told that future would come about partly through women poets I would have been even more surprised. But it had. And it did. *Think of the letters that we write our dead*, is a line from Dana Gioia's moving poem "Unsaid." It seems especially appropriate here.

Nevertheless, at that stage of my life, the connection between women and Latin remained shadowy. Even though, in a limited way, with my books at my table, I enacted it. Later I would wonder at the testy words of Bernard Mandeville, a Dutch author and physician in the seventeenth century, offering his opinion in "An Essay on Charity and Charity-Schools." There is no reason to suppose his views were not, by and large, the mainstream ones. "There are many examples of women that have excelled in learning," he concedes. "But this is no reason we should bring 'em all up to Latin and Greek . . . instead of needle-work and housewifery."

The reasons for his views aren't hard to find. Among the constructs which societies claim and hold fast and seek to control the concept of womanhood is at the forefront. Historically and culturally, it is always an intellectual property. Within that concept, certain things remain oppositional. Latin and women are one of them.

Or so I thought until I read Jane Stevenson's path-breaking book *Women Latin Poets: Language, Gender, & Authority from Antiquity to the Eighteenth Century*. Her arguments extended an invitation to think again: not just to unwrite the old histories of exclusion and omission. But to re-write certain things in a more rigorous and affectionate way. For instance, those portions of an intellectual European history which overlooked the existence of this encounter.

The book was itself a revelation and a warning. It reached

from the late Roman Republic and early empire to the complicated territories—both physical and metaphysical—inhabited
by Sarah Wiston and Susanna Wright in the new American
colonies. It came up to Phillis Wheatley, for whom Latin was a
fragile bridge slung between her American and African origins.
It took in the cartographies of anonymous medieval Latin lyrics, written in the voices of women, but not necessarily by
them. It directed a searchlight across the High Middle Ages,
from the eleventh to fourteenth century, when almost all the
women writing poetry in Latin were in religious orders.

This was the revelation. The warning was to dyed-in-the-
wool assumptions. There are always examples that challenge
set-in-stone ideas of the poet; especially the woman poet.
Anne Bradstreet is one. She is a paradigm of the contradiction. She left a high literary culture for a Puritan ethos. She
put behind her the richly marked books of a post-Elizabethan
culture. She traded the cadences of Spenser and Drayton for
the plainspoken aphorisms of the hymnal. She exchanged
meadows and orchards for harsh New England winters. The
outcome, one would think, would be an inevitable decline.
Yet her work grew steadily towards freedom and confidence.
It is a mystery within a contradiction.

Now here was a similar puzzle. The medieval woman poet,
writing in Latin, was in a very real sense double-dealing. On
the one hand, Latin was the language of conquest; of admission to the inner circles of fine learning. On the other hand, a
woman writing in that language in medieval times was using
the currency of a power she could never share; she was enact-
ing an authority she could never, because of gender, actually
claim. Jane Stevenson summarizes the problem. "In a very
wide variety of contexts, elite culture in Europe," she writes,
"has included individual women's voices while denying the

rights of women in general." But times change. Perceptions change. "Classicism's failings have become modernity's virtues," writes the fine Auden scholar Nicholas Jenkins. The failings and virtues of that long-ago time offer some unique instruction.

And so I was left with a question. In my school days I had come to understand and admire Horace and Virgil. I had come to relish the agility of the language they mastered. But that knowledge did not help me here. Who were those women, deep in a faith-bound Europe in the tenth and eleventh centuries? How could I find them? I tried to imagine the freezing convents, the walled-in beliefs. But there I faltered. I thought of Moya Cannon's line: *a ghost track carries a ghost train.* Those poets used the language of an old empire and a dominant Church. Latin was shaped by a sense of property and sharpened by defining a legal system. Yet these were women without legal rights or property entitlements.

For all these reasons, the path back to them is not well marked. To start with, they wrote in forbidding times. Many of them wrote at a moment described by a later Italian writer, Lorenzo Valla, as "a century of lead and iron." Even Helen Waddell described the epoch as one of the "nadirs of the human intellect."

Yet these women—most of whom were anonymous but a few named and celebrated like the Benedictine canoness Hrotsvitha—were alive only a century before the more visible scholar Heloise. When I try to imagine their vitality, their learning, a fragment of a contemporary Irish poem helps me see them: I think of Eiléan Ní Chuilleanáin's lines from "St. Mary Magdalene Preaching at Marseilles": *The secret shroud of her skin: / A voice glittering in the wilderness.*

But then everything grows dark. There are too many missing pieces. These were women of faith. They lived in the mystery of submission and obedience—something our age finds hard to recover. They handed over their will and their being. They would have recognized the question compellingly asked in Fiona Sampson's poem "Communion": *Is it you—or I— / I pass / and cannot see?* The truth is we can hardly recognize them. What's more, their obscurity proves a point. There is just no denying that access to a Latin woman poet in the tenth century is more difficult than access to a male poet a century later. The troubadours are romantic and familiar. A woman living in a convent, writing in a language she cannot claim and will never own, is not.

And so these Latin women poets become almost impossible to retrieve from their closed world. Perhaps we are to blame. Often enough we translate a poem: only rarely do we translate a poet. And yet looking at a text, reading an account of a woman writing at that time, we have to keep asking: How can we find a way back?

The issue is broader than the survival of Latin. It concerns the whole poetic past. It also touches on the women who were hidden in and hurt by that past. It raises the question of the relation between the two; and the causality from one to the other. For a contemporary woman poet it is a flawed, rewarding, exasperating relation. That is, if she wants to find and understand other women poets; which I did.

But even here there are problems. There is no ordained transmission of texts and contexts. There is almost the opposite. As far as women poets are concerned, the poetic past is full of vacancies, silences: it is a girl sitting in a school library learning a language she cannot imagine will one day be a language of imagination for other women. It makes it all the harder to achieve insight into a woman poet from that past. To reach—in Sandra Gilbert's eloquent phrase from her sequence "Belongings"—*the light of her mind that felt that thought that knew.*

But I was determined to find out more. I wanted to reach these strange, important poets. Trapped in an inhospitable century, their witness was all the more vital for being held hostage to power and secrecy. Surely no past was irrecoverable. All that was necessary, I was sure, was to go to that past with questions and sympathies. In other words, to keep an open mind. I was certain of that because on one occasion I had signally failed to do so.

II

I was eighteen. I had just finished my first year at university. I was a restless student, avoiding lectures and missing tests. Now, instead of studying for the autumn exams, I looked for summer work. I quickly found it in one of the new hotels being built near Ballsbridge.

It was a low-paid housekeeping job, reflective of the time. Dublin was changing. New buildings were going up. A new financial horizon was just beginning to appear. There was money in tourism. As I went in daily to my job, I was simply a fraction of a small economic expansion. The Irish summer disappeared into the noise of unfinished construction. The old trees outside, sycamores and chestnuts, had a daily skin of cement dust.

It was my job to put stationery into drawers, to close or open windows, to answer questions from the guests. Looking back, I find I've retained only a few details. I remember raw, bright corridors—a new experience for someone from a city of Georgian and Victorian shadows. And yet I have reason to remember one afternoon when I was called to a room. Perhaps there was a need to change the stationery. When that happened, the guest was usually not there. But this guest was actually still in the room. She lay in bed in the bright, jerry-built interior as if ill or resting.

She was small, fragile. The epithet *bird-like* seems right. Her hair was cropped. Her speaking voice was more English than Irish, with a high-toned Anglo-Irish shadow across it. At this distance in time, I have no exact memory of her face. But I remember the room and the late sunlight. We began a conversation. I was young and talkative. I would have done the same with any guest.

Like everything else, every other detail of that afternoon, my memory of the conversation is compressed. But here, suddenly, we were talking about poetry. She mentioned that she wrote it. Had published several books and won some awards. Herbert Read had thought a great deal of her once, she said. Recently, things had not gone so well. She felt isolated. Years later, I realized she had been talking about exclusions of gender as well as nation.

I sat in a chair by the window, glad to be talking. The green trees flourished behind me on their way up Pembroke Street. The drills and earth-movers drowned out traffic. The first gleams of a new industrial Ireland were emerging. It advertised itself as progressive, open, welcoming fresh ideas and new money. And yet in the old nation, primitive of heart and new to its freedom, this woman in front of me had found no place.

I must have told her I was a poet. And yet there was nothing mutual or properly engaging in my attitude. In my secret mind, I shrank from her talk of disappointment. I could make no sense of her harsh retrospect on loss and exclusion. I kept my counsel, or I like to think I did. More likely I postured with all my eighteen years on show. And inwardly I assured myself that whoever this was, I would never be like her.

Her name was Sheila Wingfield. She was a poet. She had been born in England in 1906 of an Irish mother and an English father. It was a background she would later describe in these words: "this duality was often a puzzle to myself." She had married in Ireland and lived between Wicklow and Offaly. If I could return to that room now—as I often wished later I could—I would be more appreciative of another and rarer dual identity: she was both a woman writer and an Irish modernist.

In the empty spaces that would open around me when I became a working poet, it would seem there were no women. No footprints. No presences. No afterlives. But there were a few. They were flawed presences. But they existed. Given the statistical odds, it was an astonishing turn of fate that I, as a young Irish woman poet, should find myself in a hotel room talking to one of my only predecessors. She had a story to tell me. I had a future to promise her. But the conversation never happened.

For all my chatter, I was tongue-tied. I did not know how to shape the necessary questions. I did not know how to seize on a simple fact. That she was a woman who had written poetry in my country. Instead, I sat there, uncomprehending. If I talked at all, I fear it was about myself. My ambitions. My future. What I would do when I left university. I did not know how to sit in front of her and say: *Tell me who you are. I need to know.*

I didn't say that to her. I didn't know how. Nor did I listen to what she told me. That missed conversation was a warning and instruction. It cautioned that there is little purpose in going to the past—or in discovering the women poets within it—without knowing what to say once you get there. I made up my mind in later years that if I found a past where a woman poet spoke, I would not go there again without the ability to listen.

I have never forgotten I failed that conversation. I could say the failure came from youth and ignorance. But it went deeper. My first sense of being a poet was anxious and canon-based. It depended on some imprecise feeling of exemption from the ordinary life of a woman. I wasn't able to talk with a poet who drew her identity, even in part, from her disappointments as a woman. I missed seeing—in Marilyn Hacker's words from her poem "Year's End"—"how lives are braided."

Adrienne Rich has written of the "perfect hour of talk." There is always a hope that a poet might meet another poet—across time or generation or difference—and have this happen. For any poet this is the dream of a poetic past. As a woman poet, it was mine: To stand in a room, in a century, at a moment. To speak plainly to a writer who does not know you, but whose work you value. To find a woman who may dress differently, who will think differently, who lives in another era. But whose purpose and hope are finally the same as yours: to write a poem that transcends difference. I was in that room. I did not have that hour. I learned that the opportunity does not return.

III

The poetic past opens up to questions. But, like Ali Baba's door in the rock, it needs the right words. When an era is as remote as the tenth century, it's hard to know what words could have that power. For myself, I wanted to know more about the women poets of the time. But the obstacles were immediate and daunting.

To start with, most of these women were anonymous. Their histories disappear down freezing corridors. They vanish into abbeys and convents where silence was the rule. Questions become whispers in those shadows. But fortunately, some questions can shape themselves into those appropriate words. This is what poetic translation does. This is what I wanted to do: by translating an extraordinary poem from that time I hoped to open a fraction of that past.

One of the most interesting comments made by Jane Stevenson concerns a ghost-poem of the Middle Ages. Its name is *Foebus Abierat*. It was written in northern Italy towards the end of the tenth century. It is both austere and erotic; an early Gothic evocation of a spirit-lover. If *The Lament for Art O'Leary*, hundreds of years later, is an oral elegy for a visible lover, this is a written lament for an invisible one.

The writer is anonymous. Jane Stevenson retains some doubts but hints at authorship: "This may be the dramatization of a pre-existing fiction . . . or what it seems to be, a highly original poem by a woman, since its writer could perfectly well be a nun." Despite its lack of a signature, *Foebus Abierat* stayed with me. When *Poetry* magazine had a translation issue a year or so later and invited me to contribute, I chose this poem to work with. If there was another poetic translation in English, I was not aware of it.

I chose it despite its obstinate mystery. Written in Latin at the end of the tenth century, and in the voice of a woman, it describes a meeting with a spirit-lover. By any standard, the poem is extraordinary in its description of the event. It is rapid, passionate; a quick arc of sounds and meaning, done in sprightly, rhymed couplets and in a language which does not usually bend to speed. Its edges are burned by vision rather than explanation. Who wrote it? And why? We will never know.

Foebus Abierat is a dream-vision lyric, composed in what used to be called "Church Latin." It is far removed from the classical Latin I struggled with, my pencil between my teeth, my teacher getting ready to scold. This was a world away. The old language is present, but a skin of liturgy and sorcery has been laid over it.

In fact, the poem as we know it barely survived. The Cambridge University scholar Peter Dronke, who wrote about it in the mid 1960s, describes the original text in the Vatican library as "mutilated." Nevertheless, he pays tribute to the work "as one of the most remarkable poems in Medieval Latin . . . [I]t achieves a beauty which is rare in a learned language."

From the first stanza, with its moonlight and wild beasts, it's clear that the agenda is magic rather than measure. Here is a poet provoking contradiction just as Anne Bradstreet does; as Sheila Wingfield might have if I had listened. The author of *Foebus Abierat* writes in the language of a high civilization. But the classical references rest uneasily in this post-barbarian world of wolves and spirit-lovers.

Phoebus was gone, all gone, his journey over.
His sister was riding high: nothing bridled her.
Her light was falling, shining into woods and rivers.
Wild animals opened their jaws wide, stirred to prey.
But in the human world all was sleep, pause, relaxation, torpor.

At the center of the poem is a passionate, impossible tryst. A man returns to his lover in the dark. He is weeping and back from the dead. Moonlight drenches the encounter: a cold light that suits the icy skin and shadow-kisses of the meeting. This is not the civil romance of Catullus. Nor the satirical version of Horace. This is an eroticism shadowed by the legendary woods and weather of northern Europe. The wild animals are already there, jaws open. The moon rises, not like a huntress, but as a light-system that reveals tragedy.

One night, in an April which had just gone by,
The likeness of my love stood beside me suddenly.
He called my name so quietly. He touched me gently.
His voice was drowning in tears. It failed completely.
His sighs overwhelmed him. Finally, he could not speak clearly.

I shuddered at his touch. I felt the fear of it.
I trembled as if I knew the true terror of it.
I opened my arms wide and pressed him against my body.
Then I froze: I was ice, all ice. My blood drained into it.
He had fled. Here was my embrace—and there was nothing in it.

Foebus Abierat may come from a lost age. But its theme is contemporary and unsettling. It suggests that the ghost-lover outside the woman might be a ghost-emotion inside her. That the borders of an external passion strongly resemble the inward contours of dream. Something like this happens in Jill Bialosky's powerful collection *Intruder*. In the poem of the same name, a woman drives through a park in autumn. A man turns to see her. In this poem, as in *Foebus Abierat*, there is a dissolving of inner and outer worlds:

He had no name, no shape,
no voice, no familiarity with anyone she knew.
She had to face the fact that he was in her dreams

In the spirit of a poem that was of its age, I tried to translate *Foebus Abierat* to ours. I followed its incantations tonally rather than rhythmically. I tried for a plainspoken note so as to make more contemporary the wonderful, long-ago cry of a woman finding and losing a body and soul; all in an instant.

I did so, knowing that translation remains one of the best questioning devices we have. It is in many ways the conversation that does not fail; the encounter that cannot be lost. And I did so remembering another lost encounter and a different failed conversation. The two events had something in common. We go to the past with our language, our knowledge, our yearning to coax it out of its essence. But it remains as it is: stubbornly gone, and hopelessly finished. If we wish to find it, even for a moment, we have to be prepared to listen, as I was not prepared to do in that hotel room. Even then, for all our visitations of language and longing, the questions keep coming back. What is the poetic past? What rights do we have over it? How can we go there?

Destinations

Letter to a Young Woman Poet

I wish I knew you. I wish I could stand for a moment in that corridor of craft and doubt where you will spend so much of your time. But I don't and I can't. And given the fact, in poetic terms, that you are the future and I am the past, I never will. Then why write this? It is not, after all, a real letter. It doesn't have an address. I can't put a name at the top of it. So what reason can I have for writing in a form without a basis to a person without a name?

I could answer that the hopes and silences of my first years as a poet are still fresh to me. But that in itself is not an explanation. I could tell you that I am a woman past middle age, writing this on a close summer night in Ireland. But what would that mean to you? If I tell you, however, that my first habitat as a poet is part of your history as a poet: is that twentieth century full of the dangerous indecision about who the poet really is. If I say I saw that century's influence in the small, quarrelsome city where I began as a poet. That I studied its version of the poet and took its oppressions to heart. If

I say my present is your past, that my past is already fixed as part of your tradition. And that until we resolve our relation to both past and tradition, we are still hostages to that danger, that indecision. And, finally, that there is something I want to say to you about the present and past of poetry—something that feels as if it needs to be said urgently—then maybe I can justify this letter.

And if some awkwardness remains, rather than trying to disguise it, I want to propose an odd and opposite fiction. If most real letters are conversation by other means, think of this as a different version. Imagine a room at dusk, with daylight almost gone. I can do this because I associate that light, that hour, with ease and conversation. I was born at dusk. Right in the center of Dublin in fact, in a nursing home beside Stephen's Green. Big, cracking heaps of sycamore and birch leaves are burned there in autumn and I like to think of the way blue, bitter smoke must have come the few hundred yards or so towards the room where I was born.

And so I have no difficulty imagining us sitting there and talking in that diminishing light. Maybe the sights of late summer were visible through the window only moments ago. Fuchsia and green leaves, perhaps. But now everything is retreating into skeletal branches and charcoal leaves. My face is in shadow. You cannot see it, although your presence shapes what I am saying. And so in the last light, at the end of the day, what matters is language. Is the unspoken at the edge of the spoken. And so I have made a fiction to sustain what is already a fiction: this talking across time and absence.

But about what? What name will I give it? In the widest sense, I want to talk about the past. The past, that is, of poetry: the place where so much of the truth and power of poetry is stored. "Poetry is the past which breaks out in our hearts," said Rilke, whose name should be raised whenever one poet writes to another. But the past I want to talk about is more charged and less lyrical than that for women poets. It is, after all, the place where authorship of the poem eluded us. Where poetry itself was defined by and in our absence. There has been a debate since I was a young poet, about whether women poets should engage with that past at all. "For writers, and at this moment for women writers in particular," Adrienne Rich wrote eloquently in "When We Dead Awaken," "there is the challenge and promise of a whole new psychic geography to be explored. But there is also a difficult and dangerous walking on ice, as we try to find language and images for a consciousness we are just coming into and with little in the past to support us."

Then why go there? Why visit the site of our exclusion? We need to go to that past: not to learn from it, but to change it. If we do not change that past, it will change us. And I, for one, do not want to become a grateful daughter in a darkened house. But in order to change the past of poetry, we have to know what happened there. We have to be able to speak about it as poets, and even that can be difficult. Ever since I began as a poet I have heard people say that fixed positions—on gender, on politics of any kind-distort and cloud the question of poetry. In those terms, this letter can seem to be a clouding, a distortion. But poetry is not a pure stream. It will never be sullied by partisan argument. The only danger to poetry is the reticence and silence of poets. This piece is about the past and our right as women poets to avail of it. It is about the art and against the silence. Even so, I still need to find a language with which to approach that past. The only way of doing that, within the terms of this fiction, is to go back to the space you now occupy: in other words, to the beginning.

When I was young I had only a present. I began in a small, literary city. Such a voluble, self-confident place, in fact, that at times it was even possible to believe the city itself would confer a sort of magical, unearned poetic identity. At night the streets were made of wet lights and awkward angles. Occasionally fog came in from the coast, a dense space filled with street-grit and salt and the sound of foghorns. By day things were plainer: a city appeared, trapped by hills and defined by rivers. Its center was a squashed clutter of streets and corners. There were pubs and green buses. Statues of orators. Above all, the cool, solid air of the Irish Sea at every turn.

The National Library was a cold, domed and friendly building. The staircase was made of marble and formed an imposing ascent to a much less elaborate interior. Old books, shelves and newspapers crowded a huge room. The tables were scarred oak and small lamps were attached to the edge of them and could be lit by individual readers. As twilight pressed on the glass roof where pigeons slipped and fluttered, the pools of light fell on pages and haloed the faces above them.

I read poetry there. I also read in my flat late at night. But the library was in the center of town. Often it was easier just to stay in and go there and take a bus home later. There was something about the earnest, homeless feel of a big library that comforted me.

I read all kinds of poetry there. I also read about poets. I was eighteen. Then nineteen. Then twenty and twenty-one. I read about Eliot in Paris. And Yeats in Coole. I read Pound and Housman and Auden. It was the reading of my time and my place: Too many men. Not enough women. Too much acceptance. Too few questions.

I memorized poems. I learned poetics—although I had no

use for that word. But I had a real, practical hunger nevertheless for instruction and access in the form. And so I learned
something about cadence and rhythm there. And something
about the weather and circumstance of tradition as well. If I
had known what to look for I would have had plenty of evidence of the tensions of a tradition as I read about the big,
moonlit coldness of Ullswater and the intimacy of Wordsworth's hand-to-hand struggle with the eighteenth century.
About the vowel changes in the fifteenth century. About the
letters between John Clare and Lord Radstock. "Tell Clare if
he still has a recollection of what I have done, and am still
doing for him, he must give me unquestionable proofs of
being that man I would have him be—he must expunge!"

When I came out of the library, I got on the bus and
watched for ten or so minutes as the rainy city went by. During the journey I thought about what I had read. I was not just
reading poems at this time, I was beginning to write them. I
was looking for that solid land-bridge between writing poems
and being a poet. I was taking in information, therefore, at
two levels. One was simple enough. I was seeing at first hand
the outcome of a hundred years of intense excitement and
change in an art form: how the line had altered, how the lyric
had opened out. I was also absorbing something that was less
easy to define: the idea of the poet. The very thing which
should have helped me transit from writing to being. But just
as the line and the lyric had opened out and become volatile,
the idea of the poet had drawn in, and distanced itself from
the very energies the poems were proposing.

This made no sense at all. When I read poems in the library
I felt as though a human face was turned towards me, alive
with feeling, speaking urgently to me about love and time.
But when I came across the idea of the poet I felt as if some-

one had displaced that speaker with a small, cold sculpture: a face from which the tears and intensity were gone, on which only the pride and self-consciousness of the Poet remained. I had no words for this. And yet I began to wonder if the makers of the poem and the makers of the idea of the poet could be one and the same. It was an amateurish, shot-in-the-dark thought. And yet all I could do was ask questions. What other way had I of dealing with a poetic past whose history I didn't know, and a tradition composed of the seeming assurance that only those it confirmed and recognized would ever be part of it? Besides I felt my questions would bring me, if not to the front, at least to the back entrance of this formidable past. But if these were the gates, who were the gatekeepers?

Stay with the fiction. Imagine the light is less. That we can no longer see the water drops and wasps under the fuchsia. That the talk continues, but in a more mysterious space. I know when I was young I could barely imagine challenging the poetic past. It seemed infinitely remote and untouchable: fixed in place by giant hands.

And yet what a strange argument I am about to make to you: That the past needs us. That very past in poetry which simplified us as women and excluded us as poets now needs us to change it. To bring to it our warm and fractious present: our recent decades of intense debate and excited composition. And we need to do it. After all, stored in that past is a template of poetic identity which still affects us as women. When we are young poets it has the power to make us feel subtly less official, less welcome in the tradition than our male contemporaries. If we are not careful, it is that template we will aspire to, alter ourselves for, warp our self-esteem as poets to fit.

Therefore we need to change the past. Not by intellectualizing it. But by eroticizing it. The concept that a template of poetic authority can actually be changed, altered, radicalized by those very aspects of humanity which are excluded from it is at the heart of what I am saying. And yet these ideas are so difficult, so abstract that I sense them dissolving almost at the point of articulation. If you were not in a make-believe twilight in an unreal room in a fictive letter, you might ask a question here. How can you eroticize a past? My hope is that this story—this strange story—will make it clearer.

When I was seventeen years of age I found myself, as many teenagers do, with time to spare between graduating from school and getting ready for college. Three months in fact of a wet, cool Irish summer. I lived in Dublin. In those times it wasn't hard to get summer jobs. So I got a job in a hotel just over the river on the north side of the city. I worked at housekeeping in the hotel. I carried keys and straightened out the rooms. The job was not difficult and the hours were not long. The hotel was placed above the river Liffey and it was right at the end of one of the showpiece streets of Ireland. O'Connell Street. Its bridge, the widest in Europe, had once been a claim to fame when Dublin was a garrison city. On this street a group of Irish patriots in 1916 had taken their stand against British rule in Ireland. They had established them-selves at the post office just above the river. The British troops had shelled the building. The position had fallen after a week of struggle and bloodshed. The patriots in the post office had been arrested and several of the leaders had been shot.

It was not hard when I was young to get off the bus on a summer morning beside a sluggish river that ran into the Irish Sea, and walk straight into Irish history. There was the post office. Inside it was the bronze statue of Cúchulain with a raven on his shoulder. Here was the stone building and the remembered action. And all up the street, placed only fifty yards or so apart, was statue after statue of Irish patriots and orators. Burke. Grattan. O'Connell. Parnell. Made of stone and bronze and marble and granite. With plaques and wreaths and speeches at their feet. I got off the bus between the river and the hotel. And I walked past them—a seventeen-year-old girl—past their hands, their gestures, their quoted eloquence, all the way to work.

There was a manager in the hotel. He was a quietly spoken middle-aged man. He looked after all the inventory in the hotel and he sat in an old-fashioned office with a ledger and a telephone. One day one of the other girls there, a bit older than I was, told me something strange about him. She told me he had a wound which had never properly healed. Every day, she said, he went up to his room and dressed it and bandaged it. And I was fascinated in a horrified sort of way, by the contrast between this almost demure man, with his dark suit and pinstriped trousers, wearing the formal clothes of small daily ceremonies, hiding his damaged secret.

But what I remember now is not exactly what I'm describing here. And that wounded man is only one part of the story. And the whole of the story is maybe not something I will be able to tell, not because I knew that man. Because I didn't. I spoke to him once or twice. Not more. Once I waited with the voyeuristic curiosity of youth, of which I still feel ashamed, at the top of the stairs to see him climb up to his room to dress that wound. But I never knew him. And never really spoke to him.

The story is something different. It has something to do with realizing that I could change the past. With going in every day to work in that hotel. With having my imagination seized, in a fragmented and distracted way, by a man whose body had not healed. And then, when the drizzling summer day was coming to an end, it had something to do with going out into the long, spacious street and walking down it to the river. Which also meant walking past the statues which had not moved or changed in the day. Which still stood on their columns, above their grandiose claims. It meant leaving the hotel with one idea of a manhood which had been made frail in a mysterious way and walking down a long well-lit street where no such concession could ever be made. Where manhood was made of bronze and granite and marble. Where no one's thigh or side had ever been wounded or ever could be. But where—so intense was my sense of contrast—I could almost imagine that the iron moved and the granite flinched. And where by accident and chance I had walked not only into history, but into the erotics of history.

The erotics of history. In a certain sense I discovered my country by eroticizing it: by plotting those correlatives between maleness and strength, between imagination and power which allowed me not only to enter the story, but to change it. And yet at seventeen my own sexuality was so rudimentary, so unformed that neither I nor anyone else would have thought it could have been an accurate guide to the history I inherited. In fact, it served. I walked down that street of statues, a girl who had come back late to her own country. Who lacked its language. Who was ignorant of its battles. Who knew only a little about its heroes. And yet my skin, my flesh, my sex—without learning any of this—stood as a subversive historian, ready to edit the text.

If you and I were really there in that room with the air darkening around us, this would be a good place to stop. To be quiet for a moment. And then to start again. This time with another question. Is it possible to eroticize a poetic tradition in the way in which I eroticized my own history? Maybe the real answer to this is the most obvious one. The only way of entering the poetic tradition, of confronting its formidable past, is through a living present. And yet it hardly seems possible that the painful, complex, single present of any one poet could offer a contest to a tradition. Despite that, what I am about to tell you, is how I discovered it. Just how tentatively I put together my sense of being a poet with my sense of a past that did not offer me an easy definition for it. And how, in a house on a summer night, with sleeping children, when I wondered how to do it, I would think back to those summer mornings, that long street with its iron orators. Of looking up, made subversive by alternative senses of power and weakness. Of how I asked myself: Would I ever be able to eroticize this tradition, this formidable past, stretching back and reaching above, so that I could look up confidently. Could I make the iron breathe and the granite move? When did I discover the past? Perhaps the answer should be, Which past?

My sense of it as a problematic poetic terrain came late. All through my first years as a poet it was just the place where poems I loved had been written, where patterns had been made which invited an automatic reverence I could not give. And so I continued to turn to that past to read those poems, but never to be part of the tradition they belonged to.

But when I married and had small children, when at last I lived at a distance from any poetic center, things changed. I started to have an intense engagement with every aspect of writing a poem. So much so, that the boundaries between the edges of the poem and the limits of the world began at times to dissolve. I was fascinated by the page in the notebook on the table, with a child's cry at its perimeter and the bitterness of peat smoke at its further edge. I loved the illusion, the conviction, the desire—whatever you want to call it—that the words were agents rather than extensions of reality. That they made my life happen, rather than just recorded it happening.

But what life? My life day to day was lived through ordinary actions and powerful emotions. But the more ordinary a day I lived, the more I lifted a child, conscious of nothing but the sweetness of a child's skin, or the light behind an apple tree, or rain on slates, the more language and poetry came to my assistance. The words that had felt stilted, dutiful and decorative when I was a young and anxious poet, now sang and flew. Finally, I had joined together my life as a woman and a poet. On the best days I lived as a poet, the language at the end of my day—when the children were asleep and the curtains drawn—was the language all through my day: it had waited for me.

What this meant was crucial. For the first time as a poet, I could believe in my life as the source of the language I used, and not the other way around. At last I had the means to challenge what I believed had distorted the idea of the poet: the belief that poetry had the power to dignify and select a life, instead of the reverse. That a life, in other words, became important only because it was the subject matter for a poem.

I knew from everything I had read that the poets who changed the tradition first had to feel they owned the tradition. Instead, I had come slowly and painfully to a number of hard-won positions which did not feel like ownership. First and foremost, I wanted to feel that whatever I lived as a woman I could write as a poet. Once I did that, I felt there was a fusion, a not-to-be-denied indebtedness between those identities: the woman providing the experience, the poet the expression. This fusion in turn created a third entity: the poet, who not only engaged in these actions, but began to develop a critique about them.

This critique may have had its origin in the life of a woman, may have begun in the slanted light of a nursery or a kitchen, but its outcome was about something different. It was about the interior of the poem itself: about tone, distance from the subject, management of the voice. It was about the compromised and complex act of language. It was about the historic freedom of the poet, granted right down through the tradition—the precious and dignified franchise—to return to the past with the discoveries of the present. And then to return triumphant to the present with a changed past.

I did not have that sense of entitlement. The interior sense that I could change poetry, rather than my own poems, was never exactly there. But if the tradition would not admit me, could I change its rules of admission? Either I would have to establish an equal relation with it, or I would have to adopt a submissive posture: admiring its achievements and accepting its exclusions. Yet what tools had I to change the resistances I felt around me and within me? Certainly neither intellectual nor theoretical ones. Gradually I began to believe that the only way to change a tradition was to go to the sources which had made it in the first place: But what were they? Intuitively I felt that the way to touch them was by reaching back into my own imagination, attempting to become not just the author of the poem but the author of myself. The author, that is, of myself as a poet. This in turn meant uncovering and challenging that elusive source of authoring within the tradition which had made not only the poem, but also the identity of the poet.

Who makes a poetic tradition? Who makes the idea of the maker? "We are accustomed to think of the poet," wrote Randall Jarrell ironically, "when we think of him at all, as someone Apart." But customs have to be made. They have to be stored deep in the culture and layered into habits of thought in order to change from custom into customary. Wherever the custom had started, I was certain it was a damaging, limiting one.

Of course it's arguable that I felt this because I was not an author in that past: neither named nor present. But I don't think so. The truth was that in my reading—scattered and inexpert as it was—I had picked up a fault line: something strange and contradictory which I began to follow. Obviously the language I use now is not the outcome of the perceptions I had then. Back then I was young, badly read, just beginning. Nevertheless, I know now that the fault line stretched from the end of the Romantic movement to the end of modernism. That it marked and weakened a strange, confused terrain of technical widening and ethical narrowing. Just as the line and the lyric began to grow plastic, open, volatile, the idea of the poet contracted, became defensive, shrugged off links with the community.

Here, for instance, is T. S. Eliot:

> We can only say that it appears likely that poets in our civilization, as it exists at present, must be *difficult*. Our civilization comprehends great variety and complexity, and this variety and complexity, playing upon a refined sensibility, must produce various and complex results. The poet must become more and more comprehensive, more allusive, more indirect, in order to force, to dislocate if necessary, language into his meaning.

Our civilization. The poet must. This was too pure for the warm, untidy enterprise of imagination as I understood it. What exactly was our civilization? Why should a poet try to reflect it in a dislocated language, instead of finding a plain and luminous one for standing outside that civilization?

Further back again. Here is Matthew Arnold, seeming to claim for an art the devotions of a sect.

We should conceive of poetry worthily, and more highly than it has been the custom to conceive of it. We should conceive of it as capable of higher uses, and called to higher destinies, than those which in general men have assigned to it hitherto. More and more mankind will discover that we have to turn to poetry to interpret life for us, to console us, to sustain us. Without poetry our science will appear incomplete, and most of what now passes for religion and philosophy will be replaced by poetry.

What higher destinies? What civilization? I repeat these questions only because it seems to me they have something to do with the fault line I spoke about. To read through nineteenth-century poetry, even haphazardly, was to become an eyewitness to the dissolution of the beautiful radicalism of the Romantic movement—where individualism was an adventure which freed the poet to experiment with the self—into a cautious and rigid hubris. Perhaps a sociologist or a historian could explain how the concept of the poet became mixed with ideas of power which had too little to do with art and too much to do with a concept of culture shadowed by empire-building and conservative ideology. And how in the process men like Arnold and Eliot accepted the task of making the poet an outcome of a civilization rather than a subversive within it.

Whatever the causes, the effect was clear. Poetry in the nineteenth century developed an inconsistency which was not resolved in the twentieth. Modernism appeared to be openly anti-authoritarian. "It was not a revolt against form," said Eliot, "but against dead form." But this apparent anti-authoritarianism was built on the contradictions of an authoritarian idea: of the poet as part of our civilization and called to higher destinies. The fault line lay here. The poets of the first part of the twentieth century had dismantled a style: they had not dismantled a self. Without the second, the first was incomplete.

Darkness. No trees. Not even outlines. Just the shadow of a profile and the sense of someone speaking. Let me remind you who I am: a woman on a summer night writing a fictive letter from a real place. Suppose I were now to turn a harsh light on my own propositions, and say why should a great tradition—an historic tradition of poetry—be held accountable to the criticisms of a woman in a suburb?

The answer is simple: However wrongheaded my criticisms, I—no less than any poet who lifts a pen and looks at a page—became an inheritor of tradition the moment I did so. The difference was that as a young woman I did so in circumstances which were relatively new. Not in the London of coffeehouses. Or in Greenwich Village. Or even in the city that was four miles away. But in a house with small children. With a washing machine in the background. With a child's antibiotic on a shelf and a spoon beside it.

And the fact is the words of poets and canon-makers—but more canon-makers than poets—had determined the status of my machines and my medicine bottles. They had determined the probable relation between the ordinary object and the achieved poem. They had winnowed and sifted and refined. They had made the authority of the poet conditional upon a view of reality, which then became a prescription about subject matter. They had debated and subtracted and reduced that relation of the ordinary to the poem so that it was harder than I thought proper to record the life I lived in the poems I wrote.

Gradually, it became apparent to me that the ordained authority of the poet had everything to do with permission granted or withheld. Not simply for subject matter, but for any claim that could be made for it. I came to believe that in that nineteenth century where Matthew Arnold proposed his higher destinies, the barriers between religion and poetry had shimmered and dissolved. The religion *of* poetry had ensued. Out of that had come a view that the poem made the experience important; that the experience was not important until the poem had laid hands upon it. I needed to challenge that.

Somewhere in that century, it seemed to me, if I could find it, would be a recognizable turning point, where the poet failed to distinguish between hubris and history. And to which I as a poet—as well as other poets from new and challenging constituencies—needed to return: to argue and engage.

No light at all. Stars somewhere. And if this were a summer darkness in Ireland the morning would already be stored in the midnight: visible in an odd brightness to the east, over towards the Liffey and the heart of the city. I have finished talking. I have to finish also with the fiction of your company, and I am surprised at my regret. Nevertheless, this letter is full of irony and hope. The hope is that you will read in my absence what was shaped by the irony of your non-presence. Despite the fact that this room, with its darkening window and summer shadows, has only been made of words, I will miss it.

Occasionally I see myself, or the ghost of myself, in the places where I first became a poet. On the pavement just beside Stephen's Green, with its wet trees and sharp railings.

What I see is not an actual figure, but a sort of remembered loneliness. The poets I knew were not women: the women I knew were not poets. The conversations I had, or wanted to have, were never complete.

Sometimes I think of how time might become magical: How I might get out of the car even now and cross the road and stop that young woman and surprise her with the complete conversation she hardly knew she missed. How I might stand there with her in the dusk, the way neighbors stand on their front steps before they go in to their respective houses for the night: half talking and half leaving. She and I would argue about the past. Would surely disagree about the present.

Time is not magical. The conversation will not happen. Even writing this letter to you has been flawed by similar absences and inventions. And yet there is something poignant and helpful to me in having done it. If women go to the poetic past as I believe they should, if they engage responsibly with it and struggle to change it—seeking no exemption in the process—then they will have the right to influence what is handed on in poetry, as well as the way it is handed on. Then the conversation we have had, the letter I am just finished with, will no longer have to be fictions.

What is more, the strengths that exist in the communal life of women will then be able to refresh and renew the practice and concept of the poetic tradition. Thanks to the women poets in the generation before mine—poets such as Adrienne Rich and Denise Levertov—many of those strengths were there when I started out. But I believe words such as *canon* and *tradition* and *inheritance* will change even more. And with all that, women poets, from generation to generation, will be able to befriend one another. And that, in the end, is the best reason for writing this letter.

INDEX